The Heart of the Matter

The Heart of the Matter

Using Standards
and Assessment
to Learn

BEVERLY FALK

HEINEMANN • PORTSMOUTH, NH

Heinemann
A division of Reed Elsevier Inc.
361 Hanover Street
Portsmouth, NH 03801–3912
www.heinemann.com

Offices and agents throughout the world

The author and publisher wish to thank those who have generously given permission to reprint borrowed material:

Figure 7–1: "Early Childhood/Generalist" was reprinted with permission from the National Board for Professional Teaching Standards *Certificate Overviews*, July 1998, all rights reserved.

Gabriela Mistral's prose poem "Llamado por el Nino (The Call for the Child)" found on the dedication page was first recited at the United Nations in New York City, in a worldwide radio broadcast in 1946.

Special thanks to NCREST for allowing the use of figures, quotes, and student material.

Library of Congress Cataloging-in-Publication Data
Falk, Beverly
    The heart of the matter : using standards and assessment to learn / Beverly Falk.
        p. cm.
    Includes bibliographical references and index.
    ISBN 0-325-00280-0 (paperback)
    1. Education—Standards—United States.   2. Educational evaluation—United
States.   I. Title
    LB3060.83 .F25 2000
    379.1'58'0973—dc21

                                                                                00-039538

Editor: Lois Bridges
Production: Lynne Reed
Cover design: Jenny Jensen Greenleaf
Manufacturing: Deanna Richardson

Printed in the United States of America on acid-free paper
04 03 02 01   RRD   2 3 4 5

Muchos de las cosas que necesitamos pueden esperar
El nino no.
Ahora es el momento en que sus huesos se estan
Formando,
Su sangre se esta haciendo.
Y sus sentidos se estan desarrollando.
A el no podemos contestarle "Manana."
Su nombre es "Hoy."

Many of the things that we need can wait.
Not the child.
Now is the moment when her bones are being formed,
her blood is being made
and her senses are being developed.
We cannot answer her with "Tomorrow."
Her name is "Today."

Gabriela Mistral

This book is dedicated to all the educators, parents, and concerned citizens who work to transform schools into places where children do not have to wait for tomorrow to experience powerful and joyful learning.

Contents

Acknowledgments

The ideas, understandings, and practices in this book have developed as the result of rich learning partnerships that I have been most fortunate to have in the course of my professional life.

I am deeply indebted to my former colleagues at the National Center for Restructuring Education, Schools, and Teaching (NCREST) at Teachers College, Columbia University—especially Linda Darling-Hammond, Ann Lieberman, Maritza Macdonald, and Suzanna Ort—for challenging my intellect and helping me to deepen my understandings about school change.

If my Teachers College colleague Lucy Calkins had not approached me a few years ago to collaborate with her on the book *A Teachers' Guide to Standardized Reading Tests: Knowledge Is Power*, I might never have embarked on this project. Lucy's appreciation of my knowledge, her respect for teachers, and her model of skillful writing helped me to envision the possibility of authoring my own book. I thank her for that as well as for leading me to my Heinemann editor, Lois Bridges. Lois' continued support, gentle prodding, and thoughtful feedback on this project has been invaluable.

To the educators with whom I have worked over the years, those who tirelessly engage in the daily acts of hope that some refer to simply as teaching, I express my gratitude for making images of possibility come alive about what schools can and should be: my fellow pioneers at the Bronx New School, especially Susan Gordon and Susan MacMurdy; my colleagues at P.S. 84, especially Barbara Goldman, Linda Margolin, and Ruth Schroeder; all of the New York State teachers whose work informed the development of the *New York State Early Literacy Profile*; my friends in communities of learning across the country whose inspirational work was articulated as the Basic School philosophy by the late Ernest Boyer, especially those in the Northeast Independent School District of San Antonio, Texas; my colleagues Ronnie Mann and Lorraine Scorscone, with whom I have worked on the UFT Teachers Center National Board of Professional Teaching Standards project; and my fellow New York City/New York State school reformers who struggle daily to improve public education.

The work of other colleagues—both personal and distant—has also informed my thinking and touched my heart. Among those to whom I am indebted are: Patricia Carini, James Comer, Miriam Dorn, Eleanor Duckworth, Hubert Dyasi, Cathy Fosnot, Michael Fullan, Howard Gardner, Edmund Gordon, Mary Hebron, Elisabeth Hirsch, Deborah Meier, Luis Moll, Jeannie Oakes, Ray Pecheone, Vito Perrone, Seymour Sarason, Theodore Sizer, Thomas Sobol, and Lillian Weber.

In the course of my many years of teaching, I have had the privilege of being a part of the learning journey of many students. I deeply appreciate all that I have learned from them.

And finally, I am grateful to my friends and family for their continual love and support. Most of all, I thank my husband, Alan, who shares my dreams for a better world and enables my work; and my daughters, Luba and Meryl, whose love is a source of inspiration for all that I do on behalf of children.

Preface

As I write this manuscript, children in the schools of our nation are completing several months of intensive testing. Test scores are being published in the newspapers, reported out by district, by school, and, in some states, even by class. Headlines proclaim "Failure!" and "Poor Performance!" Cries for "higher standards" and "accountability" ring out from politicians, federal agencies, and state education departments, reverberating in local school boards, district offices, and schools. States threaten to shut down or take over low-performing schools. District superintendents and school principals fear being removed from their jobs. Teachers anticipate with dread the reprisals that may come as a result of their students' scores. Children worry about being held back in their grade or, in an increasing number of states, whether their school's battery of required tests will keep them from graduating high school and moving on.

The heat is on most intensely in urban districts that have large concentrations of students who are poor and who come from ethnically, culturally, and linguistically diverse backgrounds. These populations, due to their lack of access to resources and other educational opportunities, as well as to tests' limited ability to accurately reflect student progress, have historically had disproportionately greater percentages of low scorers on standardized tests. Affluent and suburban districts too, however, are not exempt from pressures associated with tests. Because families often choose the community in which they live based on the quality of its schools, and because test scores are the measure most often used by the public to ascertain school quality, the desirability of a neighborhood—and hence its property values—are tightly linked to its district's test performance. Scores are scrutinized by school boards, business councils, and real estate agents, placing neighboring districts in competition with each other, generally disadvantaging those districts that include children from diverse backgrounds.

Test pressures like these are experienced in the classroom by an overwhelming emphasis on test preparation. In Texas, where the TAAS (Texas Assessment of Academic Skills) is administered to every third- through twelfth-grade student and has high-stakes consequences for students, teachers, and administrators, test preparation frequently begins in kindergarten, replacing instruction in some schools for an entire half day of each week throughout the school year. Across the nation in New York State, in the weeks prior to the administration of the state's new fourth-grade English Language Arts test, many fourth-grade classes also devoted most of their class time to test preparation activities. In one school district that I visited during this period, a principal lamented to me about how test prep this year had replaced the rich studies that had been going on at the very same time last year: Reading, book talks, writing, research, book making, plays, trips, and schoolwide presentations of student work were abandoned in favor of page after page of test-prep worksheets.

Well-meaning efforts to ensure that all children achieve high standards—defined as doing well on high-stakes tests—have led, in many places, to the reinstitution of practices that research of the last few decades has advised us can be detrimental to student learning: mandated lockstep curricula, testing in the primary grades, ability tracking, or overreliance on basal readers and whole class instruction. These initiatives, while intended to strengthen the coherence of the educational experience for students across a grade or a school, have the unintended consequence of being either developmentally inappropriate, of creating inequitable learning experiences, or of spelling out in such detail what teachers should do—when and in what order—that they constrain the creativity, inquiry, and decision making needed to keep teaching fresh, responsive, and professional.

In the midst of this frenzy of standards, testing, high-stakes accountability schemes, and media and political pressure, it is a struggle for educators to stay focused on what we know is important: teaching that creates genuine understandings and teaching that encompasses the wholeness of children's growth and development. It is a struggle not only to preserve our commitment, but also to sustain school environments that nourish this kind of learning—teaching the way that children learn, that builds on diverse strengths, that stimulates inquiry and reflection, and that nurtures caring in our classrooms and our schools.

This book offers a guide for how to stay focused on teaching and learning in the context of these complex times. Based on my years of experience as a school-based educator, my involvement in the conception and design of large-scale, standards-based, performance assessments, as well as on the research that I and colleagues have conducted on schools successful at supporting diverse learners, I try, in the pages that follow, to "unpack" the ideas and initiatives that are part of the current movement for standards-based reforms. My aim is to help us make sense of the complex issues that are involved, to explain the concerns of the various perspectives that are influenced and affected by these initiatives, to separate what is useful from what is harmful, and to offer a pathway for how to proceed.

I suggest how to define standards that are worthy, how to make worthy standards explicit and meaningful in teacher/school–developed curricula, how to create performance assessments that embody these standards and inform teaching, as well as how to use standards and performance assessments to enhance professional learning. My purpose is to deepen our knowledge base so that we, the teaching profession, will feel empowered to act and speak out on behalf of the children whom we care for and teach. Too often our voices, our knowledge, and our expertise are overpowered by the voices and actions of others whose purposes are far away from the educational matters that are the foundation of our work in schools. I write this book in the hope that it will contribute to clearer understandings of the complex issues that so critically affect what we do. I hope that the thoughts and information contained within will help those who closely interact with children to participate avidly in the educational conversation, will enable us to advocate for policies that genuinely support the children whom we serve, and, most importantly, will help us to enact practices that stay focused on what I believe is the heart of the matter: teaching that supports powerful learning for *all* the children in our nation's schools.

The Heart of the Matter

Chapter 1

What Gets in the Way of Important Learning

Problems of Tests and Testing Practices

When I was the director of a public elementary school, each spring's administration of standardized tests brought anxiety to me and my colleagues. Because the test scores then, as they are now, were the loudest voice in the public conversation about teacher and school accountability, we felt under considerable pressure to make sure that our students were able to perform well.

From our perspective, however, these tests provided only a limited, and sometimes misleading, view of students' proficiencies and their progress. The test questions offered students little opportunity to use higher-order thinking, to problem solve, or to apply knowledge to real-world problems. The lack of contextualization for the questions often disadvantaged those from culturally and linguistically diverse backgrounds. With "right" or "wrong" answers as the only options, students' answers to test questions gave us little indication of their thinking or the strategies they used in their learning. The response options in the multiple-choice format distracted children from conveying what they understood and did not take into account their sometimes logical explanations for the choices they made. Overall, information provided by these tests gave us little understanding of what students knew and what they could do that we could use in our teaching.

These shortcomings of standardized tests, documented in numerous studies and analyses (Archbald and Newmann 1988; Darling-Hammond 1989, 1991, 1994b; Darling-Hammond, Ancess, and Falk 1995; Edelsky and Harman 1988; Resnick 1987; Sternberg 1985; Wiggins 1993), were particularly problematic for students like Akeem, a third grader whom I tutored for several years as he struggled to gain literacy skills. When I first knew Akeem, his nationally normed reading scores indicated that he was among the least proficient readers of students in his grade. Yet, even when he began to improve as a result of the

supports he received in our school—when he began to master the range of cue-
ing systems that were needed for making meaning out of print, when he was
able to successfully challenge an increasingly wider scope of materials and texts,
when he began to persist instead of giving up in the face of difficulty—his test
scores essentially remained the same. Because such tests are designed to compare performance with others, rather than demonstrate the degree to which a
student has mastered specific criteria, they did not reveal Akeem's actual
progress. Although he had improved, so had his peers; so his scores gave the ap-
pearance that he was standing still.

This way of evaluating Akeem's learning was particularly frustrating to me
and Akeem's teachers because *our* evaluations of his progress indicated that he was
indeed developing as a reader and writer. We noted his changes through a variety
of evidence collected in classroom contexts over time: documented observations
of his reading, lists of books that he read during the year, and samples of various
types of writing. This data showed us what Akeem could do, revealing his
strengths as well as his weaknesses. It also offered us information about *how*
Akeem was approaching his learning. It helped us to shape our instructional
strategies so that we could be responsive to his specific needs (Falk 1994).

My colleagues and I were troubled by the discrepancies between our school's
way of evaluating student learning and the evaluations provided by standardized
tests. We recognized the need of a district and state to have information about students' progress for accountability purposes, yet we did not understand why the
system's methods of evaluation could not utilize some of the assessment strategies
that gave us such rich understandings of our students' learning. We wanted tests
that would support, not be at odds with, the ways we taught and the ways our students learned.

It was the vision of Akeem and others like him that led me, over the years,
to seek alternatives to existing tests that better reflect student progress and that
provide more useful information than those generally used. In the course of this
work, I studied the history of testing and principles of measurement. I examined
assessments from all over the world to find out what possible models existed in
order to utilize the lessons of their experiences. I learned about assessments used
in other systems that do not have such great disparities between how children
learn and how they are tested (Darling-Hammond et al. 1993; Eckstein and Noah
1993; Lewy 1996; Mitchell 1992; Rothman 1995; Valencia, Hiebert, and Afflerbach 1994).

In this chapter I present some of what I have learned about testing in the
hopes that by sharing it with you, my readers, you too will be armed with some of
the knowledge and information that is needed to make meaningful change in this
arena. This chapter includes information about how testing rose to the position of

prominence that it currently occupies in our educational system and how it reflects the perspective on learning and on education's purposes that has predominated throughout the history of public education in this country. I examine the nature of standardized tests, their qualities and characteristics, as well as the issues, problems, and limitations of testing that challenge us to seek better ways to evaluate student progress.

Testing: Its History and Purpose

The testing emphasis that is so pervasive in our country as we enter this new millennium has its roots in the birth of our public education system. Tests and their accompanying accountability mechanisms have been used in the educational agenda over the years to address society's fluctuating economic, political, and social needs. Each change has reflected prevailing views about what constitutes education's purpose, the nature of the teaching profession, and what effective school management and successful change look like.

Economic Influences on Schools and Testing

Formal, written, standardized tests were introduced into United States schools during the late nineteenth century, when Horace Mann's "common school" brought public education to more citizens than had ever before been the case. As our country shifted from an agrarian to an industrialized society, schools reflected these changes too. Compulsory school attendance laws, combined with waves of immigrants during the early part of the twentieth century, led to larger and more diverse school populations. Henry Ford's invention of the factory assembly line and Frederick Taylor's concepts of scientific management, both of which were revolutionizing industry to more "efficiently" produce greater quantities of better-quality goods, influenced the design and nature of schools. The one-room schoolhouse of the farming era was replaced by the industrial era's "factory model" school, functioning in much the same way as the assembly line in America's fledgling industries. It housed huge numbers of students in large buildings, sequenced them from one grade to another, circulated them from classroom to classroom, regulated them with bell schedules and time clocks, instructed them through a programmed series of textbooks, and monitored them with standardized tests to efficiently keep track of their learning (Darling-Hammond 1993).

Just as the industrialization of our economy influenced the design of schools and the proliferation of testing, it also impacted public views about the purpose of education. The purpose of schools for many was seen as fulfilling society's needs to efficiently produce workers who have sufficient skills to enable the businesses that employ them to compete successfully with each other and within global markets. Public schooling thus generally focused on "training" the broad masses to acquire the basic knowledge and skills they would need to perform their menial jobs in the factories. Only a smaller elite group was needed to acquire the higher-level understandings and skills that would be needed to effectively manage over others. Special groups, or tracks, in public schools were developed for them or, more often, they attended private schools (Tyack 1974).

Although this view of the purpose of schooling has held sway over public thinking and public investment in education over the decades, a contrasting view has competed with it from time to time. This latter view, originating in the early part of the twentieth century with the work of philosopher and educator John Dewey, is that schools should be places committed to helping all individuals learn to think deeply, realize their potentials, and live democratically in order to vitalize public life (Dewey 1916).

These two different views have dominated public thinking in alternating decades throughout United States public education's history. Although Dewey's child-centered philosophy of democratic schools flourished in the early 1900s, in the 1930s and 1940s, in the late 1960s, and once again in the school reform era of this last decade, the workforce preparation view of schools' purpose has generally exerted a stronger influence over the years. The "factory-model school" has been the norm for public schooling in America. From its inception, it has sought and used new advances in "scientific" teaching, measurement, and testing.

Tests were seen then, as they are now, as a scientific and improved way to help teachers and the public know whether teachers were accomplishing what was expected of them. Tests were also used to organize increasingly large and diverse school populations into grade levels and to sort them into programs according to "ability." In this way, tests determined who would get access to what type of curriculum.

Advances in test technology have occurred over the years to enable schools to use tests for this purpose of determining who gets what kind of education. Among the first of these was intelligence testing, introduced to our country at the turn of the twentieth century by Alfred Binet, a French psychologist. He designed a "mental age" scale that was intended to identify students unable to benefit from instruction. The scale was adapted in the United States by Lewis Terman, who transformed it into an easily administered paper and pencil test that provided an intelligence quotient, better known as IQ. This test, along with a similar one known as the Alpha-Beta test developed by the U.S. Army for recruitment in World War I, was used on a broader scale with all kinds of individuals to evaluate their inherent abilities and then to make decisions, on the basis of those abilities, about the kind of educational opportunities they should have.

Although some have heralded this kind of testing and its subsequent variations as an effective way to allocate educational opportunities or to improve the ability of schools to meet students' needs, others view tests as gatekeepers to educational opportunities and as barriers to social and economic advancement (Darling-Hammond 1997; Glaser and Silver 1994; Tyack 1974). They argue that the way tests have been and continue to be developed creates and sustains the dominance of some societal groups over others. Pointing to the fact that test scores of those from society's dominant groups have historically outperformed those from nondominant groups, they reference evidence that suggests how tests have been deliberately designed to ensure the continuation of this trend. One example is from the history of the development of intelligence tests. When the earliest versions of intelligence tests were being constructed, females far outperformed males. Given the era's attitudes about women's inferiority, this discrepancy was unthinkable. So many of the test questions—those on which the women performed well—were removed from subsequent versions of the test until the final version verified that males excelled in what was considered to be acceptable proportions (Darling-Hammond 1994b, 1997).

A similar process happened when tests were being developed in the early part of the twentieth century for the purpose of determining who would have access to the limited opportunities for schooling and jobs. When test performance of certain immigrant groups was high and threatened to jeopardize the jobs or school places of those groups who traditionally held positions of dominance, the tests were redesigned to ensure that not too many immigrants (according to the status quo of the time) would get into the sought-after positions.

And so it came to be that test results have historically and consistently demonstrated the rich outperforming the poor, native English speakers outperforming immigrants, urban dwellers outperforming rural dwellers, and whites outperforming blacks. "Evidence" from test results was even used at one time to argue that Indians, Mexicans, and Negroes should be segregated in special classes and that Jews, Hungarians, Italians, and Russians were "feebleminded" and should be restricted from entering this country. Test "evidence" has been used to "prove" that intelligence is hereditary, reinforcing already prevalent social notions that some groups are superior to others (Kamin 1974; Oakes 1985).

Although such interpretations and uses of tests were called into question as early as the 1920s, and although numerous testing experts have continued over the years to caution against this kind of misuse of test results (Glaser and Silver 1994), unfair and inappropriate testing practices persist to this very day. Biases are still found in test items and test "evidence" continues to be relied on as a major source of information for making decisions about students' school futures. Despite obvious and important social and economic inequities that affect students' test performance, tests are still used to group students by levels of ability or to differentiate curriculum for vocational or college-bound students. Tests all too frequently track disproportionate numbers of poor, immigrant, and minority children into low-level courses or special education programs (Darling-Hammond 1991; Gordon 1999; Oakes 1985).

The Influence of Behavioral Learning Theories

Coinciding with the development of the view that economic needs drive school practices, and at the same time that testing became embedded into the very fabric of public schooling and life, a theory of learning emerged at the turn of the twentieth century that both influenced and justified these phenomena. At this time the field of psychology was first evolving as a discipline to explore human learning and behavior. To do this, many psychologists studied animals in experimental contexts. Since they found that a stimulus followed with reinforcement could get rats and other animals to perform specified behaviors on command, they reasoned that humans functioned in similar ways. This led them to formulate what has become known as the theory of behaviorism, a theory that conceptualizes learning as an incremental process of mastering increasingly complex skills and that advocates teaching methods that emphasize practice and repetition of these skills reinforced by punishments or rewards (Skinner 1954).

Although much has since been learned about human learning that has led to the development of other theories challenging the assumptions of behavioral psychology, behaviorism is a theory that today still heavily influences psychology as well as teaching. The programmed instruction found in many basal readers, workbooks, and curricular materials is based on behavioral theory. Tests' heavy reliance on short answer, fill in the blank, or multiple-choice formats also stems from a behavioral stance. Because behaviorist perspectives view learning as primarily skill mastery and the accumulation of individual bits of knowledge, it logically follows that short answer, fill in the blank, or multiple-choice questions can effectively evaluate if learning has indeed taken place.

The influence of behaviorism on education is not confined only to teaching methods, however. It affects school curricula and accountability structures too. It is seen in the "direct instruction" used in many classrooms and in the standardized curricula that is being mandated in many schools. It is the driving force behind the high-stakes consequences that are associated with test performance. It is the raison d'être of the top-down bureaucratic structures that administer many districts around this country. The idea behind all of these practices and approaches is that learning and behavior can be controlled by sequencing events and structures appropriately and by securing outcomes through sanctions and rewards.

While this behavioral theory of human learning may produce immediate demonstrable results, it is a theory that is based on control and on a lack of belief in the innateness of human strivings to learn and grow. Behavioral theories negate the capacity of intrinsic motivation to stimulate and harness learning. They ignore massive bodies of evidence that have been accumulated from studies of the brain and human learning that reveal learning to be an active, social, and uniquely individual process in which each individual constructs understandings based on connecting new information with prior knowledge (Piaget and Inhelder 1970; Resnick 1987; Sprenger 1999; Vygotsky 1978).

New learning theories such as these suggest that the standardized teaching, testing, and schooling that are rooted in behaviorist conceptions of learning actually get in the way of creating environments supportive of the learning needs of our diverse student population.

Limitations of Standardized Tests

Think for a moment about the kinds of tests that you have experienced in your learning life. Chances are, what most readily comes to your mind is an image of timed paper and pencil tests that had high stakes attached to their outcomes: the battery of reading and math tests that were administered each spring to your classes in elementary and middle school; the SATs and other College Board entrance exams that determined what type of college you could get into; discipline-based school completion exams that you had to pass in order to graduate.

If you are like me and other people I know, taking such tests caused you great anxiety. And the scores you achieved may not have been an accurate reflection of what you knew. Your performance on these tests may even have aroused feelings of inadequacy or humiliation. Some of the reasons for these reactions can be understood by examining the nature of the tests as well as the constraints they present. Let us look deeper at these issues from the perspective of Akeem, the struggling third-grade reader I worked with long ago.

Tests Show What Students Do Not Know— But What About What They Can Do?

Tests generally measure only one kind of learning and one kind of demonstration of that learning. They often do not accurately reflect what test takers know and can do. This was especially true for Akeem because of the powerful role that interest played in his ability to demonstrate—or not demonstrate—his skills.

In his classroom and at home, Akeem had begun to pore over books he cared about. He especially loved books about trains. He knew everything there was to know about subways—the names of all the different lines, where they went, how they connected to others throughout the New York City subway system. He often spent weekends riding the trains with his mom and little brother. Books on trains totally engrossed him. He brought his own images, stories, and associations to their pages.

Unfortunately, Akeem's increasing ability to read in areas that interested him was not revealed on standardized tests. He could not find anything of interest in the unrelated passages he was called upon to read. He had trouble focusing on the passages and engaging his mind on the topics. These problems were not unique to him. I, too, remember having difficulty concentrating when reading over some of the passages on the very same test that he took one school year. One passage was about sixteenth-century European architecture; another was a technical passage on the chemistry of filmstrip development. Like Akeem, I had little interest in either of those topics. As a result, I had difficulty focusing and an equally hard time answering the questions.

But these were not the only problems that made tests difficult for Akeem. The test format was also distracting and confusing to him. The reading test in our district at that time was what is called a cloze test: It consisted of paragraphs that test takers were required to read in which there were words omitted and left as blanks; the test taker was directed to choose (from a multiple-choice list on the page at the side of the paragraph) the correct word that belonged in the blanks. This kind of test was confusing to Akeem. Even though his teachers had introduced him to the format in advance, and even though they tried to prepare him by practicing similar types of paragraphs repeatedly, the entire experience of reading on this test was so unlike the reading he had begun to do with such emerging competence in his classroom that he got frustrated and intimidated and was unable to effectively marshal his efforts to perform well.

Test Bias

Witnessing Akeem go through the experience of taking this and other tests made me sensitive to still other problems of standardized tests. I also began to see how the content of tests often does not reflect or capture the diversity of test takers' backgrounds or experiences. Because test questions may contain assumptions and facts that are grounded in the context of the dominant culture, they fail to include forms of knowledge that are relevant and of interest to people who are from other backgrounds or who have had other kinds of experiences. This places test takers who are from nondominant cultures at a disadvantage in demonstrating what they know and can do (Darling-Hammond 1995).

Akeem's test experiences made me aware of how many tests are, in a sense, a test of background knowledge more than they are a test of ability. For example, in order to get the gist of the passages that Akeem encountered on the reading test mentioned above, he needed background knowledge about subjects that he knew little about. He would have been aided greatly in answering the European architecture questions if he had known about Europe and its history or understood more about concepts related to time. He would have been helped on the passage about filmstrip development if he had some familiarity with cameras and how film is developed. Yet he, unlike students who come from more resourced communities, did not have a family that had traveled abroad; he did not have shelves of books in his home about people and places from faraway lands; he had never adjusted the focus of a camera lens, never made his own slides or videotape. He *did* have knowledge about other things, however. Give him something to read about the New York City subway system or any of his other interests—fish had become his latest passion—and you would see a different reader than the reader he was when taking this test. His interests and knowledge base simply did not match the knowledge base required to negotiate the test (Falk 1994).

This mismatch between the content of what appears on many tests and the experiences of many test takers was not unique to Akeem. I remember once hearing one of my colleagues, who is of Hispanic descent, talk about a reading test he had encountered as a child growing up in the southwest. He described a test passage that was about maple trees, a type of tree he had never seen in his native desert environment. He recalled how he had difficulty answering the test questions not because he could not read the words, but because he had no idea what the content of the test passage was about (Calkins et al. 1998).

In addition to how test content is often biased toward the knowledge and background of certain cultures, bias is also evident in the language that is used on tests. Many nationally used standardized tests contain questions on grammar and language usage or they evaluate grammar and language usage in students' extended responses to test questions. Often what might seem correct to a child whose first language is not "conventional" English differs in syntax and structure from what is deemed correct on the test. The English language learner has to do much more to be correct than those children whose cultural and linguistic backgrounds are similar to those of the test. The English language learner has to "code switch" into a different language and way of thinking and demonstrate not only that she can decipher the words in the passages, but that she can answer the questions in the language of the test.

These subtle and not so subtle cultural, linguistic, and socioeconomic biases that are found in many tests impact test scores of many students who come from diverse backgrounds. In fact, socioeconomic, racial, and linguistic differences are highly correlated with differences in test performance. For example, for many decades the National Assessment of Educational Progress (a nationwide exam that keeps track of national trends in student learning) has shown that test takers from poor and minority backgrounds do not perform as well as test takers who are white and middle class (NAEP 1981). Understanding the nature of test design begins to explain figures such as these.

But the bias of tests is not limited only toward differences in socioeconomic, racial/ethnic, or linguistic backgrounds. People with different learning styles or "intelligences" that differ from those emphasized on tests often do not perform well either. These test takers can make errors that have little to do with their knowledge. Rather, they choose "incorrect" answers simply because they bring a different sense of logic or way of thinking to the test-taking process. This happens especially with young children. It is not uncommon, for example, for children to answer this frequently asked test question wrong: *Which is the best title for the story?* This question assumes that there *is* one best title and that all individuals will respond to it in the same way. But there can be many different ways of determining what constitutes a "good" title. What might seem to be a good title to me might not seem to be a good one to you. The "error" may have far less to do with the test taker's lack of knowledge or ability than it has to do with his or her personal taste or creativity.

Problems with Multiple-Choice Formats

A related problem experienced by test takers is the multiple-choice format of standardized tests. This was certainly the case for Akeem. The response options of the multiple-choice format sometimes confused him or even distracted him from selecting the "correct" answer. Oddly enough, this is exactly what multiple-choice questions are designed to do. They contain answers that are either partly right, that might jog the memory of a related experience, or that could be right if looked at in a particular way. The test makers call these partially right answers "distracters." They are intended to do just that.

A well-known example of this kind of question was written about in Miriam Cohen's *First Grade Takes a Test* (1980). This is the story of a young child's first experience with a reading test. The test asked children to read short passages and then answer multiple-choice questions about each one. One of the test questions, following a passage about rabbits, asked for a description of the kind of food rabbits like to eat. The correct answer, according to what was written in the passage, was *lettuce.* However, neither this answer nor any of the other available response options listed *carrots,* which corresponded to what the child knew from her experience feeding the class rabbit. So she penciled the word *carrots* into the text booklet, ignoring the options offered by the test. Of course she got that question wrong. But her incorrect answer had nothing to do with reading ability. She could read the passage perfectly (Calkins et al. 1998).

Now we all know that one of the skills that reading tests test is to identify information and discriminate what is important from the text. But we also know that in our everyday reading lives, indeed our learning lives, we draw on all that we know in order to make sense of what we read. Good teachers regularly encourage children to do this. Only during a test will children read texts that deliberately set out to penalize them for constructing meaning by drawing on their prior knowledge. When tests restrict the response options solely to those offered in a multiple-choice format, children may make mistakes that have little to do with lack of knowledge or inability to use a skill. In reality, the "mistake" may only demonstrate the test's inability to provide an opportunity for the child to demonstrate what she knows.

Multiple-choice questions have still other limitations: They have little capacity to measure test takers' abilities to think deeply, to create, or to perform actual tasks. They do not generally provide test takers with the opportunity to demonstrate how to wrestle with complex, ambiguous problems, to structure tasks, or to produce ideas—the kinds of skills and abilities needed in order to be successful in life and schooling (Darling-Hammond 1991; Harris and Sammons 1989; National Research Council 1982; Resnick 1987; Sternberg 1985).

Many believe that these problems with tests are trade-offs that one has to accept in order to have an "objective" measure of what people know and can do. But just because standardized tests are designed to have "right answers" that are determined in advance and can be scored without ambiguity does not mean that they are really "objective." Yes, they may be easier and seemingly more objective to score. But the stories and discussion above illustrate how this way of measuring knowledge is far less "objective" than one might think.

Tests Are Poor Diagnostic Tools

Because tests provide only a limited measure of a narrow aspect of learning, they are generally poor predictors of how individuals perform in other settings. Even the sacrosanct SAT has been revealed to be a predictor of performance only for the first-semester work of students who enter college. And that prediction is only accurate for 50 percent of those individuals who take it (National Center for Fair and Open Testing 1999).

An assessment story shared by one of my students in a graduate course on performance assessment provided a good example of the predictive abilities of standardized tests. It is a story of how Eli became a certified scuba diver. The certification process for scuba diving involves completing a certain number of course hours as well as passing two tests: a paper and pencil test and a set of scuba diving tasks. Here Eli discusses how the written test inaccurately reflected what she could do:

> Though I had earned a perfect score on the quiz asking me what I would do if my air were to run out, when I actually experienced this situation—my instructor snuck up behind me (in the deep end) and turned off my air supply—I was not prepared for the anxiety I felt and did all the wrong things. I shot up to the surface and gasped for air, despite the fact that I knew this would have seriously injured my body had we been in deeper water. (Jannes 1995)

In much the same way that Eli's written test was a poor predictor of how she would apply her theoretical knowledge, many paper and pencil tests do not demonstrate how individuals tackle challenges or what abilities they rely on in order to solve a problem. When only final answers are recorded and when these results are reported solely in numbers, the figures do not provide enough information about areas of competency or difficulty to inform instructional strategies or to give a sense of how the test taker really is doing. These kinds of tests provide little information that can help you to improve. You either pass or fail; you rank in the "good" percentiles or the "bad." But you never quite know why you scored as you did.

Standardization: Problems and Possibilities

Given all of these problems with standardized tests, why do we use them? Why can't we rely on teachers—those closest to students' learning and who know students best—to tell us how students are progressing in their learning?

Although teachers' assessments of individual students are a critical part of good teaching, they are not sufficient if we want to look at student progress across groups or classrooms, schools or districts. And looking at student progress across groups is necessary if principals, superintendents, and state education commissioners are to ensure that students are learning what they need to know and receiving the resources and supports that are needed to do this well. To obtain this important information, we need to have a means of evaluating similar things in comparable ways. To do this, some kind of common measure is required.

Take, for example, this situation: Suppose two third-grade children from different schools in a district are considered "accomplished" in reading. But these schools have very different populations—one that has students who are predominantly poor and one that is mostly middle class. What evidence does the district superintendent (the person responsible for assuring the quality of learning in the district) have that the programs these students experience in both places are providing them with quality teaching and the supports that they need? How can the superintendent get a sense of how the students in both places are doing?

There are many rich ways to assess the quality of teaching and learning that goes on in schools. Among the different aspects that need to be examined are a school's teaching practices and resources; student attendance, drop out, and graduation data; teacher qualifications, attendance, and retention rates. But student performance is also an important indicator. And while it ideally should be looked at through a variety of forms of evidence, some kind of common measure that can fairly evaluate and easily report progress is needed as one part of a strategy to ensure that all children have access to quality education. Some kind of common measure that can be looked at across contexts and individuals can be useful to help guard against our culture's deeply ingrained biases about people from different racial and socioeconomic groups that frequently lead to different treatment, fewer opportunities, and lower expectations for some. In light of these realities, a common measure for keeping track of student progress across different groupings makes sense. Using some common measure of progress that contains the same expectations for all students can be one part of a way to challenge everyone to have similar expectations for all children and thus to provide them with equal opportunities so that they can all have a chance to meet those expectations.

So—developing some common (standardized) ways to evaluate progress can be a mechanism to provide information that can help in efforts to ensure equity in our schools. At the same time, however, standardization also creates a set of dilemmas and challenges that can undermine equity and be cause for concern. How can we fairly measure very different people in very different contexts in exactly the same way? How can we standardize the measurement of such a complex thing as learning, which we know is highly dependent on context and individuality?

The process of standardizing a situation to test a skill or specific bit of knowledge does inevitably create problems. Standardizing a situation can alter it significantly. A standardized task or problem on a test frequently ends up testing something very different than what it originally intended to measure. For example, test standardization is commonly achieved by administering a test under the exact same conditions. Everyone takes the test on a given day, hears the same directions, reads the same passages, and has the same amount of time to complete it. In order to develop test questions that can be administered and answered under these conditions, however, the substance and process of what is being tested is restricted to what can be easily measured across large groups in a cost-efficient and timely way. This restriction limits and often distorts the nature of what is being tested. Test questions generally end up being of the paper and pencil variety, frequently posing artificial choices in formats that ask test takers to do very different things than what they do to use the same knowledge and skills in their daily lives.

The technical term for how well a test measures what it purports to measure is called *construct validity*. Because of how a construct is constrained or distorted by the process of standardizing a test, many standardized tests are limited in this regard. Indeed, standardization presents a dilemma: While needed in some way to reliably examine test takers' performance across groups, it poses serious problems in regard to maintaining the authenticity or validity of what is being assessed.

Problems and Contradictions with Norm-Referenced Tests

The problems of standardization pale, however, in relation to other factors associated with most standardized tests. Constructing tests primarily for the purpose of comparing one test taker with another, a process known as norm-referencing, is the cause for greater problems.

While finding out how students compare with others is not an unreasonable thing to want to know from a test, the problem with norm-referenced tests is how they are constructed to obtain this information. Decisions about the content of norm-referenced tests—from the nature of test questions to the difficulty level of items—are driven by the goal to sort test takers along a continuum of performance, from high to low. In order to do this, items considered for placement on such tests are pretested on a sample of students that represents all possible test takers. As a result of this pretesting, a set of items is chosen to appear on a test. Only a few test questions are placed on the test that *all students* in the pretest were able to answer and only a few test questions are placed on the test that only *a few students* were able to answer. The bulk of the items placed on the test fall in the mid-range with varying degrees of difficulty. The range of scores for those who take this test is thus determined in advance to be dispersed along a "normal" or bell curve.

The problem with this way of designing tests is that item placement is guided more by the quest to sort and rank students in relation to each other than by what is considered important for test takers to know. Sometimes items are eliminated from a test, regardless of the importance of the item's content, because too many, too few, or the wrong subset of students can produce the correct answer (Hill 1992).

Imagine you had to design a test to rank five musicians, all of whom have been studying for a year and are roughly equivalent in their overall ability but have different strengths and styles of performing. In order to determine who is "the best," you must decide that certain elements of performance will be used to discriminate among the players. One strategy that could be used might be the time it takes for a player to complete a passage. If this factor were used as the discriminator, while all of the players might be able to perform the piece, the one who could play it the fastest would be ranked first. Other important qualities of playing that are more difficult to measure, such as depth of expression, would probably not get reflected in the test. So the player who brought tears to your eyes because of her sensitive phrasing and nuancing would not be credited for this skill. She would be overlooked in favor of the player who was able to demonstrate what was most easily measurable: the speed at which the passage could be played (Calkins et al. 1998).

Besides the fact that many norm-referenced tests are unable to acknowledge what different learners can do because their differences are difficult to demonstrate in a standardized format, there are other problems with tests designed primarily for the purpose of comparison. One is that norm-referenced tests give test takers little indication about what is actually being evaluated. The criteria for success are not generally made public (most of these kinds of tests are kept secret for test "security purposes" and most often—after the tests are completed—teachers, students, and parents never see their tests again). So, for example, when we are told that our score on a particular test was in the ninetieth percentile, we often do not have the vaguest idea why we achieved that score or what that score actually means about what we are able to do. All we really know is that we did better than ninety percent of the other test takers.

This problem does not occur with a different kind of test—*a criterion* or *standards-referenced* test. In contrast to the norm-referenced test, the criterion or standards-referenced test is developed not primarily to compare performance, but primarily to determine to what degree test takers have command of specified knowledge and skills. A good example of a criterion or standards-referenced test is the Department of Motor Vehicles' driving test. In this test, there are clear expectations that must be met—what the community has determined is necessary for all drivers to know in order to have safe streets. Everyone knows what these expectations are, everyone can prepare to meet them, and, one hopes, everyone will master the skills needed to meet the expectations to pass the test.

Clearly articulated expectations and criteria (i.e., standards) for what constitutes success on any given test gives all test takers a fairer chance to achieve the goals than when test criteria are left unexplained. Some test takers may not need this guidance because they have an inclination toward certain kinds of learning or have had sufficient experience with or exposure to a subject that coincides with the test's image of excellence. But for those whose experiences with the test content have been limited or who struggle with a particular discipline, clear criteria and articulated expectations can serve as a guide to learning and test preparation. Clear standards can "level the playing field" a bit to help individuals from different backgrounds succeed.

In contrast, norm-referenced tests tend to inhibit possibilities for test takers to succeed. As explained above in the bell curve discussion, norm-referenced tests are constructed to include questions that 50 percent of the original piloting sample got wrong. This means that the test is designed with the expectation that 50 percent of the population that takes it will get scores below the fiftieth percentile, the percentile generally designated as "grade level" or "passing." The test is thus deliberately created so that half of all test takers will fail.

Most people do not realize this about norm-referenced tests—they do not realize that when taking a norm-referenced test the cards of success are stacked against them. So schools and communities work hard at test practice in the hopes that they will beat the odds to have their students "pass" (which means they have achieved scores above the fiftieth percentile). But not everyone can score in the top half of the performers. This impossibility is guaranteed by what test makers do when too many students get high scores. The test makers either redesign tests to contain more difficult questions or they "renorm" existing tests so that the same number of correct answers yields a lower score than it did before. In these ways norm-referenced tests are created and maintained to ensure that, regardless of how proficient students are, some will always be in the bottom half of the rankings (Cannell 1987, 1989).

A comparison that may be helpful here is how the baseball rankings work: Regardless of how high batting averages become, some teams are on the bottom, even if these teams have overall averages that are much higher than those from previous years. While the teams in the bottom rankings may actually improve their performance from year to year—possibly more than those teams in the upper rankings—their improvement generally goes unnoticed because the criterion for success is not the amount that any one team has improved, but which team scores higher than the others. The only statistic reported is who is the best and how others compare to that. Norm-referenced tests work in similar ways. Although low-scoring individuals may actually improve their performance on a test from year to year, their improvement is often obscured because it is reported only in relation to how others are doing. Even when low scorers improve, if other test takers have also improved, the low scorers still end up in the bottom rankings, as if no change has occurred.

Evidence of genuine progress can also be obscured when comparing the performance of schools on norm-referenced tests. For example, if the scores of all schools decrease, a school's scores could remain the same but appear to look better. Or, if all schools' performances increase, a school could improve its scores but go down in the rankings. School scores can also be affected by fluctuating attendance. For example, many schools have such highly mobile student populations that huge percentages of the students enter and leave the school in the course of one school year. Even though the test scores of these students are not really a reflection of the school's teaching, their scores affect the school's overall scores and the school's ranking in relation to others.

These kinds of problems can lead to test score reports that are quite misleading. Despite this fact, norm-referenced tests have a dramatic impact on school curricula and teaching methods. Indeed, they affect many aspects of school life.

The Impact of Testing on Curriculum and Teaching

Tests Narrow the Curriculum

Most tests we have experienced in our school lives do not reflect present-day knowledge that people learn in meaningful and purposeful contexts by connecting new information to what they already know (Gardner 1983; Kantrowitz and Wingert 1989; Resnick 1987). Conceived on the notion that "basic skills" are the foundation for "thinking skills," most tests focus on rote rather than conceptual learning. They ask for recall and recognition of discrete facts instead of a demonstration of skills and knowledge in lifelike situations.

This aspect of testing, combined with the ways that tests are used to determine high-stakes consequences, has exerted a tremendous influence on teaching. Teachers feel pressured to "teach to the test" as well as to teach in the format of the test (Madaus 1989). These pressures lead to an overemphasis in classrooms on superficial content coverage, rote drill, and memorization of discrete skills. Classwork gets dominated by testlike tasks, such as answering multiple-choice or fill in the blank questions, at the expense of work that bolsters students' proficiency in aspects of learning that are not tested, such as writing essays, conducting research, experimenting, reading and discussing literature, debating, solving difficult problems, and creating products (Boyer 1983; Cohen, McLaughlin, and Talbert 1993; Darling-Hammond 1991; Darling-Hammond and Wise 1985; Goodlad 1984; Kantrowitz and Wingert 1989; Koretz 1988; Madaus et al. 1992; McKnight et al. 1987; NAEP 1981; NAEYC 1988).

Tests Constrain Student Learning

The results of this phenomenon can be seen even on traditional measures of students' performance. Since the 1970s, when standardized tests began to be widely used in the United States for accountability purposes, basic skills test scores of students in our country have increased only slightly while scores on assessments of higher order thinking have steadily declined in virtually all subject areas (ETS 1989a; NAEP 1981). International assessments reveal similar findings—that United States students and schools do not do as well on higher order thinking and problem solving as students and schools in European and Asian countries (Mc-Knight et al. 1987; Schmidt, McKnight, and Raizen 1996). This phenomenon is attributed to the fact that other countries routinely use work samples, essays, and teacher-developed oral examinations to assess students' progress, whereas United States schools rely heavily on multiple-choice basic skills tests, texts, and teaching methods (ETS 1989b; National Research Council 1982).

A number of studies have examined the relationship between tests and the learning that takes place in classrooms. In a study that analyzed items from the twelve most widely used standardized mathematics and science tests for United States students in grades four, eight, and in high school, George Madaus and his colleagues at the Center for Evaluation and Testing at Boston College found that only 3 percent of items on mathematics tests measure such high-level conceptual knowledge as the ability to generate examples and apply concepts. Only 5 percent of the items they examined measure thinking that goes beyond simple recall and routine algorithms (Madaus et al. 1992). The researchers found that the limited conception of knowledge of these tests led teachers to teach in a rote manner even though this practice got in the way of what they believed to be worthwhile learning.

Another study found that the more teachers focused on getting their students to produce good scores for the state test, the more likely they were to use teaching practices that were considered to be "bad mathematics" (Schoenfeld 1988). Other studies confirm this phenomenon. Constance Kamii compared math test performance of two socioeconomically and racially comparable groups of second-grade students: one "experimental" group that had received instruction emphasizing understanding—they were taught with games, conversation, and materials; the other "traditionally instructed" group that had been taught with an emphasis on using procedures and the algorithm correctly—following a sequenced text and using flash cards and worksheets. In addition to examining each group's performance on multiple-choice standardized achievement tests, Kamii also administered to them a test of word problems that children were asked to solve as well as explain.

Significant differences were found in how the two groups of children performed on the two different tests. While performance was similar on the standardized multiple-choice test, it varied significantly on the test that called for constructed responses and demonstrations of how problems were solved. A striking example of how students' responses differed can be found in this sample question: "There are twenty-six sheep and ten goats on a ship. How old is the captain?" All of the "traditionally instructed" students wrote "thirty-six" as their answer, automatically adding the two numbers, despite the fact that it did not make sense. Twenty-seven percent of the "experimental" group, however (a figure that, while low, is statistically significant) noted that this question did not make sense and was unable to be answered (Kamii 1989).

Not only students' thinking abilities have been affected by testing methods that rely heavily on the use of multiple-choice and short-answer questions. Their writing abilities have been affected as well. The 1988 National Assessment of Educational Progress (NAEP) writing assessment found that only 2 percent of eleventh-grade students could write in an "elaborated" fashion and fewer than 20 percent could perform adequately on a task requiring analytic writing. Is it any surprise that most of the eleventh graders whose work was examined in this assessment (61 percent) reported that their teachers asked them to write a three-page paper less than once a month or not at all (ETS 1990; Office of Research, U.S. Department of Education 1993)?

How we waste young people's minds! At a time in their lives when they are most open to new ideas and most flexible to develop new skills, much of the time that they spend in school is devoted to memorization and drill. On a personal note, I can recall the frustration I felt when my own two daughters, during their high school careers, took courses that had curricula driven by our state's high-stakes testing system. Because the tests examined recall of a tremendous amount of information through primarily multiple-choice questions, that is what the courses emphasized—seemingly endless content coverage and memorization of countless facts. One four-semester Global Studies course covered the entire span of written history around the world. When calculating what that ambitious undertaking meant in terms of instructional time, we found that students were allotted approximately seven seconds (!) to learn about each year of recorded history.

Biology especially stands out in my mind as a memorable example of how the press for content coverage robs children of meaningful learning opportunities. Instead of focusing on the exciting ideas of this field that is rapidly changing how we live in the world, instead of providing opportunities to explore new concepts through experiments and research, my daughters spent the precious hours of their teenage years poring over study guides that asked questions like these (Darling-Hammond 1997):

> The circulatory system of the earthworm is most similar in structure and function to that of a
>
> 1. hydra
> 2. protozoan
> 3. grasshopper
> 4. human
>
> The excretory organelles of some unicellular organisms are contractile vacuoles and

1. cell membranes
2. cell walls
3. ribosomes
4. centrioles

These types of questions, unfortunately, are not unique to tests given by my state. They are common in many tests administered around the country. They reduce complex issues to right or wrong facts, making it difficult for a thinking person to choose a right answer. Here are some sample questions from a "World Studies" high school exam given in Chicago that epitomize these problems (National Center for Fair and Open Testing 1999):

Economic systems determine which one of the following?

A. what trade should take place
B. food and language
C. how much goods are worth
D. which people should be employed in certain jobs

Which of the following describes the economic system in MOST African nations today?

A. The government encourages villagers to produce enough for their own needs.
B. The government controls many aspects of business with limited private investment.
C. The government gets financial support from Western Europe to develop industry and agriculture.
D. The government controls most of the land for farming.

Isn't it hard to demonstrate understandings of such complex issues when they are presented in this simplistic format? Many of us could make a case for choosing several of these answers if given the opportunity to discuss and explain them. But that is not the way this kind of test works. The test taker has to figure out the thinking of those who created the test in order to get the answer right.

Problems with How Tests Are Used

The problems associated with standardized tests would be less problematic if the tests were used as only one source among many other kinds of information about student learning and if they were not so directly tied to high-stakes decisions about students and programs. However, tests are increasingly being used to make such important educational decisions as determining a student's track or program placement, promotion, and graduation; evaluating teachers' and administrators' competence and school quality; and allocating sanctions and rewards.

Using Tests to Place Students in Programs and Tracks

Tests scores are frequently used to place students in tracks or programs. This often happens as early as first grade, when students are assigned to instructional groups and programs according to their test scores. By junior high school, test scores are used even more extensively, often to organize schools into totally homogeneous populations. As a result, challenging curricula get rationed to only a small proportion of students who are in the top tracks. Students placed in the lower tracks are exposed to a limited, rote-oriented curriculum that, no doubt, accounts for the fact that they achieve less than students of similar capabilities who are placed in academic programs or in untracked classes (Cooper and Sherk 1989; Oakes 1985; Trimble and Sinclair 1986). These curricular differences can explain much of the disparity between the achievement of white and minority students and between the achievement of higher- and lower-income students (Lee and Bryk 1988; Oakes 1985). In these ways, test use impedes, rather than supports, the pursuit of high and rigorous educational goals for all students.

A good example of how reliance on test scores limits educational opportunities can be found by examining how tests were used in the federal Title I program. This program was created to provide supplementary resources to all students in need whose household incomes fall below a certain economic level. Title I regulations used to mandate that student performance be monitored through the use of norm-referenced, standardized tests. The results of these tests were used each year to both identify students who would be eligible to receive Title I services and to assess the progress of each student who was already in the program. In addition, scores were used to evaluate the effectiveness of the program and each teacher in it. This system of evaluation created pressures for teachers to "teach to the tests." Title I programs often devoted inordinate amounts of time to drilling students on test like tasks so that children would do well on the evaluations. Ironically, the children who were most in need of rich learning experiences ended up spending huge amounts of time practicing short text passages and answering fill in the blank questions while their more fortunate peers got to read engaging literature, write about their thoughts and experiences, take trips, do projects, and participate in other "enrichment activities."

It took years of lobbying by professional psychologists, testing experts, researchers, and early childhood educators to change the Title I legislation so that norm-referenced standardized tests would no longer be used for evaluation of students who received those services (NAEYC 1988, 1991). Despite all these efforts, however, today there is a resurgence of "teaching to the test." Although the nature and form of the tests have changed, test-prep curricula is still being force-fed to students who are most at risk of achieving "passing" scores.

Using Tests for Student Promotion/Retention

Tests have long been used as the criteria for decisions regarding the promotion of students from one grade to the next. Despite a substantial body of research that has been amassed over the years to demonstrate the negative effects of this kind of test-based decision making, this practice is making a big comeback today—from the federal government to local districts—in calls to "end social promotion." New York City's Board of Education recently passed a resolution that no student will be promoted from the third, the sixth, or the eighth grade without passing the city's reading and math tests. Nearly one third of the more than one million student population (more than three hundred thousand students) are expected to be retained in their grade this coming year!

Resolutions such as this are proliferating around the country in spite of many studies that demonstrate how retaining students contributes to academic failure and behavior difficulties rather than to success in school. Studies that compare students who were retained to students of equal achievement levels who were promoted have found that students who were retained are consistently behind on both achievement and social/emotional measures (Darling-Hammond and Falk 1997b; Holmes and Matthews 1984; Shepard and Smith 1986). Retained students consistently suffer poorer self-concepts, have more problems with social adjustment, and express more negative attitudes toward school at the end of the period of retention (Darling-Hammond and Falk 1997b). One study even found that children fear grade retention so much that they cite it third on their list of anxieties, following only the fear of blindness and death of a parent (Byrnes and Yamamoto 1986).

Grade retention has also been found to increase dropout rates. Even a single retention increases the likelihood of a student dropping out of school by 40 to 50 percent. A second retention increases the risk by 90 percent (Carnegie Council on Adolescent Development 1989; Massachusetts Advocacy Center 1988; Wehlage et al. 1989).

New York City's Promotional Gates Program, instituted and then eliminated in the 1980s, provides a case in point of the ineffectiveness of retention policies based on test scores. Gateways were created in grades four and eight through which students could pass only if they demonstrated a specified level of performance on the standardized citywide reading and mathematics tests. When students did not succeed, they were mandated to repeat the grade. But what they experienced by repeating the grade was frequently what had not been successful for them the first time. Thus, large groups of students continued to fail and were retained repeatedly. Some remained in a grade for so long that their advanced age and size caused a host of problems. Having twelve-year-olds in the fourth grade and sixteen-year-olds in junior high made teachers' jobs more difficult and produced higher incidences of disciplinary difficulties, lower achievement, and ultimately higher dropout rates. In the face of these failures the program was eventually abandoned (Gampert and Opperman 1988).

Other districts have had similar experiences. In the state of Georgia, where tests scores have been used since the beginning of the 1980s as the basis for decisions about retention and graduation, the high school completion rate in Atlanta dropped from 75 percent to 65 percent by 1982 and to 61 percent by 1988 (Orfield and Ashkinaze 1991).

These examples suggest that the practice of using test scores as the sole basis for decisions about students' educational futures leads to damaging effects on students, especially for those who are from poor and minority backgrounds. Even the test makers warn against using their tests as the basis for retention decisions. Riverside Publishing's *Interpretive Guide* to the Iowa Tests of Basic Skills (ITBS) states that it is inappropriate to use their test "to decide to retain students at a grade level." Yet each year thousands of students in Chicago who take this test are held over in their grade because their test scores do not reach the cutoff point for passing. Other cities and states are increasingly doing the same thing, sending thousands of children to rigidly prescribed summer school programs under the threat that they will have to repeat a grade if they do not pass the test at summer's end (National Center for Fair and Open Testing 1999).

Sanctions and Rewards Based on Test Results

In addition to using test results for decisions about whether students should be promoted or retained, in many states and districts tests are also used as the basis for allocating sanctions and rewards to the educators who work there. Increasingly, superintendents are getting bonuses of thousands of additional dollars written into their contracts for each year that test scores go up during their tenure. In some places superintendents, principals, and teachers are also threatened with dismissal or other sanctions if test scores do not rise or if they go down. Numerous districts and states are offering money incentives to teachers and schools who are able to achieve increases in their students' test scores. Students too are affected by the high-stakes test frenzy. In Michigan, the governor recently offered up to $3,000 in college assistance to students who pass that state's high school exam (National Center for Fair and Open Testing 1999).

Using Test Scores to Evaluate Programs
Leaves Out Many Important Matters

Position papers issued by national professional organizations such as the American Educational Research Association, the American Psychological Association, and the National Council on Measurement and Evaluation (AERA, APA, and NCME 1999), the International Reading Association (1999), the National Council of Teachers of English (1999), the National Association for the Education of Young Children (NAEYC 1991), and the National Forum on Assessment (1995) warn against using test scores as the sole basis for any decisions about students' futures. Relying only on test scores as the sole measure of a student's or school's effectiveness is fraught with problems. It ignores the fact that student learning and program quality is the result of many critical factors, of which a student's test scores is only one. Equally important to examine are the resources that go into schools and the quality of teaching that takes place. Just as when a farmer wants his pigs to grow, he doesn't only weigh the pigs, he feeds them and tends to them too—if we want our students to learn we must use our resources to do more than just test them. We must provide them with the resources and opportunities they need to be able to realize learning goals.

Using only test scores to determine how well students and schools are doing presents still other problems not yet mentioned. One problem is that test scores, in and of themselves, obscure other important issues that affect school performance. When numbers are combined or aggregated and then reported in relation to other groups, who and what is being looked at gets obscured. For example, reported scores do not necessarily reflect the fact that school and program populations change from one test administration to the next. A stable population is not necessarily being assessed. Thus, "gains" or "losses" may be a function of changes in who is taking the test, rather than how individual students actually score. This problem is particularly pronounced in schools that have high mobility rates—rates so great in some schools that they have pupil turnover rates exceeding 100 percent annually. How does this happen? By having more student entrances and departures during a single school year—individual students leaving and returning more than once or many students enrolling for only a short time before leaving—than the total number of students who are counted as the base student population.

Another issue that affects a school's test performance is the wide array of differences among the students who attend. This must be considered when evaluating how schools are doing. While some schools serve primarily students whose backgrounds are privileged, others serve student populations who have extraordinary challenges—poverty, homelessness, recent immigration, or lack of knowledge of the English language. These factors need to be taken into account when school outcomes are reviewed. Test scores alone are not sufficient to explain the reasons why a school is having difficulties or why test scores are going down (Darling-Hammond and Falk 1997a).

Test Overemphasis Causes Harmful Policies and Practices

When test scores are used as the single loudest voice in the evaluation of student and school performance, school practices and policies that can be damaging to students inevitably begin to appear. For example, incentives are created for schools to keep out students whose test scores might lower the school's average scores. There are several ways that this occurs. Because a school's average scores are sensitive to the population of students taking the test, sometimes students are left back in a grade so that their scores won't "pollute" the school's average score. In other instances, schools that select their student populations make test performance part of the criteria for admissions, so that no students who are low scorers are ever let in.

And there are still other practices resulting from test emphasis that can be damaging to students. These include referring large numbers of low-scoring students to special education or encouraging low-scoring students to drop out of school (Darling-Hammond 1991; Haney and Madaus 1986; Koretz 1988; Shepard and Smith 1986; Smith and Rottenberg 1991).

In addition to affecting the makeup of student populations, the high stakes associated with test scores create incentives for students and educators to cheat. Due to the recent rise of high-stakes tests, there have been increased reports of teachers who help students select test answers, of teachers or administrators who actually alter students' responses on answer sheets, and of administrators who circulate the actual test in the school before it is supposed to be given. Other ethically questionable practices being reported around the nation are school personnel who encourage some students to stay home on exam days, administrators who hire consultants for the purpose of helping teachers raise test scores, or administrators who pressure teachers to teach solely to the test (National Center for Fair and Open Testing 1999).

This frenzy of test preparation for high-stakes tests is fueled by the textbook and test publishing companies who market materials that promise to prepare students for the high-stakes exams. Some commercially available textbooks, workbooks, and test preparation materials are so extraordinarily similar to the tests that actually get administered (many of these materials are produced by the very same companies that create the tests) that one could make the case that their use in itself is a form of cheating (Harmon 1996). But what is more important than that, I believe, are these questions: Does such heavy involvement with test preparation really further the goal of improving student learning? Does such concentration of efforts on test preparation foster the ideas, dispositions, knowledge, and skills that we want to see developed in our students? What if we followed similar practices with, say, those who were going to take an eye test? What if eye charts were available for practice before people actually took an actual eye exam? While all of the eye chart practice might result in patients being able to read more eye charts correctly, would it reveal who really could and could not see well? Would we end up with more people who could see better? These are the questions we need to ask ourselves in relation to high-stakes testing. These are the things we need to consider if we are to stay focused on our purposes and stay true to our goals.

An additional problem created by high-stakes tests is the incentive for talented staff to opt for placements in schools where students are easy to teach. Who wants to risk losing rewards or incurring sanctions by teaching in schools where, because there are exceptionally needy students, high-performance standards are difficult to attain? Because of the high-stakes consequences of test performance, many capable and qualified teachers and administrators may shy away from working in schools that have a disproportionate number of struggling students. They may feel that the demand to prepare their students to meet test performance standards is too great for them to be able to accomplish in the one short year they have with their students, especially given many students' history of poor preparation. So the students who desperately need expert help (and, one could argue, would benefit the most from it) are left to learn primarily from those who are inexperienced or unprepared or unable to get jobs in what are considered more "choice" locations (Darling-Hammond 1997). In the nation's poorest schools, this situation is sometimes disastrous. "Thousands of children are taught throughout their school careers by a parade of teachers without preparation in the fields they teach, inexperienced beginners with little training and no mentoring, and short-term substitutes trying to cope with constant staff disruptions" (National Commission on Teaching and America's Future 1996, 16).

Incentives based on test scores thus compound the disadvantages of disadvantaged students, penalizing them twice over. The neediest students receive the least resources, the least experienced teachers, and then are punished for failing to perform as well as students attending schools with more resources (Darling-Hammond 1991; Oakes 1990).

What We Can Do

The problems discussed in this chapter about the nature of tests and how they are used are not new. They have appeared and reappeared throughout our nation's history. As the pendulum has swung between the two competing views of education and its purpose—be it the "technical" view that teaching is "telling" and its purpose is primarily to prepare individuals for their place in our economic structure or the view that learning is about creating understandings and that the purpose of education is primarily to help individuals fully develop their capacities and participate in our democracy—testing emphasis has either ebbed or flowed.

Today, our nation's current catapult into the technological/information age presents us with unprecedented challenges. It presents us with dramatically new expectations of and purposes for schools as well as ways that schools teach and assess learning. No longer is it enough for schools simply to educate only for rudimentary skills. Knowledge is exploding at such a rapid pace that it is impossible to teach all there is to know. Schools must now meet the challenge of preparing citizens who can think critically and creatively, who know how to access information where and when it is needed, who can apply knowledge and skills to real situations, who know how to problem pose as well as problem solve, and who are flexible enough to adapt to our fast-paced, continually changing world.

This proposed agenda for our schools is a mix of ideas from conceptions of schooling that historically have competed with each other. Both economic needs as well as human aspirations affect what we need from education. These require that we change not only the ways in which we teach but also how we assess what is taught.

In light of these challenges as well as newly emerging understandings about how people learn, in light of increased insights about what are effective strategies for teaching, and in light of new advances in measurement technologies that have produced assessments that are better for teaching, we have a unique opportunity to reexamine our practices, learn from our history, and move forward in how we educate students. We have evidence that points to better ways that we can use to support students' learning. Our challenge is to put our knowledge to work.

Chapter 2

A Better Way

Powerful Learning Supported by Assessment

In contrast to the way that standardized, norm-referenced, multiple-choice tests influence teaching to emphasize content coverage, fact recall, and rote performance of skills, there is another way to think about curriculum, instruction, and assessment. This way views the goals and purposes of learning as developing abilities to use critical skills and information in order to "have wonderful ideas" (Duckworth 1987)—to inquire, discover, pose, and solve problems that not only make sense of the world but that can have an impact on it. It uses assessment as a valuable tool to inform instruction and support powerful learning.

Teaching and Learning for Understanding

To attain this goal requires a departure from the *teaching as telling/learning as listening* way of doing business in schools. Instead, it provides a two-way exchange between teacher and learner, with an emphasis on *teaching as listening/learning as telling*. In this way of conceiving the learning experience, the teacher begins by connecting to students' understandings and experiences, always working to build bridges between their existing ideas and important new knowledge. Genuine understanding and the ability to apply what is learned are the goals.

A critical part of this approach to teaching and learning is ongoing assessment by the teacher. It provides important information about what each learner does and how he does it so that the teacher can know what strategies and approaches to use to be effective. It offers insights to the learner's way of thinking, why he makes mistakes that he does, what strengths the learner relies on in order to succeed, and what areas need strengthening in order to improve. This kind of teaching takes into account the learner's intentions, goals, and purposes as well as external standards and expectations. The result is, hopefully, an individual who not only achieves the community's expectations and high standards but who also is empowered to take charge of his own learning and to realize his own goals and dreams.

Have you ever experienced learning like this—learning that helped you to genuinely understand a new concept or master a new skill and that awakened you to the possibility of gaining access to still other new and wonderful ideas? Think about it for a moment. Can you recollect a time in your life when you have had a powerful learning experience? Can you remember a time, a place, a person, an incident that was responsible for helping you to genuinely learn something new? What about this experience brought you to this new understanding?

If you are like me (see my story, below), or the many students with whom I have discussed these questions, your learning story might be quite unlike the kind of learning that is generally associated with formal schooling.

Understanding Base 4: My "Aha!" Experience

Math was always difficult for me. At some point during each math course I took, I found myself at a stumbling point—a point beyond which I simply could not conceptualize. Perhaps this had to do with the fact that the teachers' primary method of teaching was *telling*. Problems and the correct method for solving them were usually presented in a lecture format, followed by in-class and homework assignments, and then end-of-unit tests to evaluate how well students had acquired the new information.

This process had something important that was missing—connection to my understandings. My confusions and misconceptions were never addressed. I did not raise them with questions or request further explanations because I was already embarrassed that I did not understand and did not want to appear even more foolish than I already felt. I thus resigned myself to rotely following the teachers' instructions so that I could get the "right answer." Assuming that math intelligence was a gift with which I had not been blessed, I soon abandoned hope of understanding what the problems were about and proceeded to develop my identity as someone who simply was not a "math person."

All of this changed when, as a graduate student in education, I took a course called "How Children Learn Mathematics." The class featured a variety of approaches to teaching that included exploring mathematical concepts with materials, examining and discussing our thinking processes, explaining our ideas in partner and group discussions, and applying skills to solve problems in projects and tasks that simulated real-life situations.

Lots of class time was given to explorations of different materials. I distinctly remember spending hours at work with "Base Blocks"—little wooden blocks that can be put together and pulled apart to represent the different columns of the algorithm—the ones, tens, and hundreds for base ten or their correlates in other bases. Although base was a concept that had been covered in my high school math courses, I had never really understood it. In this math class, however, I was continually drawn to these blocks. As I worked with them week after week—sometimes individually, sometimes in groups—they beckoned me toward the understanding that had eluded me for so many years.

At times during my work in this course I felt as if I was grasping the meaning of what I was doing. At other times I really did not. I wavered in and out and around the edges of understanding until, one evening, I had one of those "Aha!" moments when everything came together for me conceptually. As I explained Base 4 to my classmates, taking the four from the "ones" column and putting it into the "tens," I suddenly got it. I really understood how bases worked! Now effortlessly manipulating the blocks, I was able to explain the concept and the process of moving from one base to another. The number system made sense to me now in a way that I could never have imagined before!

As I reflect on this experience, I can attribute my discovery of understanding to three important aspects of the learning environment: the availability of ample materials with which we were encouraged to interact, the way that the class was structured, and the teacher's skill at helping me to connect my ideas. Each class time always included a time to explore ideas in a variety of ways and a time to talk about what we had discovered from our explorations. We were asked to explain what we had done, what we understood, where we were stuck in our thinking, what questions arose that puzzled us. The very process of explaining what we knew helped to clarify and consolidate our knowledge.

At the same time, the teacher was actively engaged in seeking to understand our intentions. She listened and observed us during our explorations. She watched and valued our mistakes, using them to help us recognize what we knew as well as what strategies we relied on in our learning. She raised questions that challenged and probed our understandings, helping us to identify our interests and ideas and to make connections to our own past learning. She continually posed new ways of looking at the same concept, taking responsibility for finding the unique pathway that could make the connection for each and every learner. Her patience and support and responsiveness to our ideas helped us to feel that through our efforts, *anything* was possible, that understanding and mastery were indeed within our reach.

Principles for Teaching the Way People Learn

Contained in this story are elements of learning that are similar to those suggested by cognitive theories as well as recent insights derived from brain-based and other educational research (Bruner 1960; Carini 1986; Cohen and Barnes 1993; Falk 1996; Fosnot 1989; Gardner 1983; Piaget and Inhelder 1970; Resnick 1987; Sprenger 1999; Sternberg 1985; Vygotsky 1978). Teaching could be more effective if these understandings were utilized more in schools:

- In-depth understanding is essential to higher-order thinking, problem solving, and performance.
- Connections between learners' experiences and the content of the curriculum need to be made for understanding to take hold.
- Opportunities to explore, inquire, discover, experiment, problem solve, or *mess about* (Hawkins 1965) with ideas, materials, and relationships facilitate the connections that develop deep understandings. Varied learning situations—projects, trips, readings, reports, discussions, field work, and internships—challenge learners to reason, question, draw connections, communicate, evaluate viewpoints, frame problems, acquire and use evidence, and create new knowledge, understandings, relationships, and products.
- Real-life situations offer important occasions for learning and for drawing connections between the separate disciplines. In the course of trying to solve practical problems, learners have continual opportunities to organize and reorganize their understandings and to develop multiple access routes to their knowledge.
- Social interaction is critical to learning. We need to talk, question, and comment with others about what we are coming to know. The questions and comments we receive from our teachers and peers expose us to different perspectives, enrich, extend, and solidify our understandings, as well as provide us with a framework to organize our thoughts. As we struggle to explain what we think, we are pushed toward greater comprehension.
- Unevenness, unpredictability, and messiness characterize the learning process. Each individual has a unique way of working out and expressing his own personally meaningful understandings. This happens

through a process of piecing together varied experiences that bridge old understandings with new ideas.

- Time is essential for understanding to take root. It often requires a period of weaving in and out of knowing that is "sometimes forward, sometimes in return, sometimes momentarily intense, sometimes bypassing" (Weber 1991, 11).
- Mistakes are valuable opportunities to gain access to learners' understandings.
- Interest is a potent motivator to understanding and to mastery. As individuals identify and follow their interests, they can draw upon them to support their learning.
- Self-esteem and effort are critical to learning. When individuals are looked at in light of their strengths, rather than defined by their weaknesses, they are enabled to do more and better work.
- Different kinds of learners learn in different ways. Individuals learn and demonstrate what they know in different ways, at different rates, and from the vantage point of their different experiences (Darling-Hammond, Ancess, and Falk 1995; Falk, MacMurdy, and Darling-Hammond 1995; Garcia and Pearson 1994; Gardner 1983; Kornhaber and Gardner, 1993).

This last point is a fact that I became aware of most poignantly through my experience as a parent. My two daughters are very different kinds of learners. My older daughter, for example, is an avid and rapid reader. When she was little she could never get enough of books and seemed to magically turn into a fluent reader at around the age of four. In contrast, my younger daughter has always preferred to draw or paint from the earliest age. She likes to slowly savor and visualize what she reads. In school-related learning one readily recalls facts and details of almost anything that she hears or reads; the other focuses instead on understanding the implications of the ideas. Though different in their approaches to learning and the way they express what they know, both daughters have unique strengths and skills. Living with them has made me acutely aware of how utilizing only one approach to learning and how assessing knowledge in only one way values some types of knowledge at the expense of others and may undermine the efforts of some kinds of learners to develop their potentials.

Building on the Strengths of Diverse Learners

If schools value the aspects of learning discussed here, and if teaching is tailored to how different learners learn, a far greater range of individuals could experience success than is currently the case. Too often, however, this does not happen. In many classrooms the focus is almost exclusively on linguistic and logicomathematical forms of knowledge, generally excluding ways of knowing and of expressing that knowing that are relied upon by many: building, drawing, using the computer, speaking, or interacting with others. As a result, students who hold interests and who possess strengths that are different from those currently emphasized in school often feel that, because there is no room in the classroom for the activities they value and for the ways of learning that they do well, there is literally no room for them either.

In contrast, when teaching is organized to look at individuals in light of what they *can* do, rather than to define them by what they *cannot* do, there *is* a place for different kinds of learners. By extending the range of what is valued in schools as well as the range of ways to learn important subjects, many more individuals—the builder as well as the writer, the artist as well as the mathematician—can experience learning success.

There are lots of examples where this has happened successfully. Generally the success stories come from schools where students with multiple talents and skills are supported through a combination of rigorous academic instruction with real-world learning experiences (Boyer 1995; Cohen, McLaughlin, and Talbert 1993; Darling-Hammond, Ancess, and Falk 1995; Falk 1994; McCombs and Whisler 1997; McDonald 1996; Newmann 1996; Steinberg, Cushman, and Riordan 1999; Wasley, Hampel, and Clark 1997; Wiske 1997). These schools break down the walls that have long existed between learning in school and learning in life. They provide students with opportunities to experience learning in ways that are commonly valued in life but that are not commonly found in schools. As a result, these schools have high attendance and graduation rates, low dropout rates, and high percentages of students who perceive school to be a place that supports them and their overall development (Bensman 1994; Falk 1999; Ort 1999).

Assessment in the Service of Learning

Approaches to learning that value differences call for approaches to assessing that reveal and value multiple talents and skills. Most existing assessments do not do that. They value a limited slice of knowledge and do not sufficiently allow for different kinds of learners to express what they know and what they can do. In fact, they actually drive teaching and learning away from those complexities of powerful and successful learning that are difficult to measure, focusing instead on lower-order skills and facts that are easier to measure (through short answers and/or multiple-choice options).

Those of us who care about supporting a wider range of learners and a more fulsome view of learning are thus faced with the challenge of finding better ways to evaluate the higher-order thinking skills and performance abilities that are the hallmarks of our goals. We need to find better ways to capture a fuller range of learning goals, to provide information that helps teachers adapt instruction to students' strengths and their needs, to inform students, parents, and the public about what students actually know and can do. We need to create or find assessments that develop students' abilities to frame and structure problems, find and generate information, evaluate and propose alternatives, invent ideas and products, and engage in messy problem solving. We need assessment approaches to help us keep track not only of *what* students know but *how* they know it so that we can use this information to inform our teaching and to support our students' learning.

Some general principles can guide us as we construct assessments and assessment systems that support and reflect broader views of learning. An overarching principle is that assessments be grounded in good teaching and supportive of meaningful learning. Because of the powerful impact that assessments have on curriculum and instruction, this point is critically important. Therefore, assessments need to be composed of worthy tasks that are faithful representations of the contexts encountered in a field of study (Darling-Hammond 1991, 1994b; Glaser and Silver 1994; National Association for the Education of Young Children 1991; National Forum on Assessment 1995; Shepard 1995; Wiggins 1993, 1998).

Make Assessment a Learning Experience

One way to ensure that assessments serve learning is to make sure that they are rich and dynamic and reveal the *process* as well as the *product* of learning. This kind of information helps teachers shape their instruction in ways that are responsive to students' needs. When assessments demonstrate the process of students' thinking, they encourage teachers to inquire and reflect—about their students, about the nature of their discipline, and about the strategies used in teaching (Falk and Ort 1998). They guide teachers, students, and their families to a better understanding of progress and growth. Assessment thus becomes a learning experience for all the participants in the process (Darling-Hammond, Ancess, and Falk 1995; Falk and Ort 1998; Shepard 1995; Wiggins 1989; Wolf 1989; Wood and Einbender 1995).

Connect Assessment to Learning Goals

Assessments that are useful to learning also provide accurate information about students—either insights to their unique learning needs and understandings or to how they are progressing in relation to desired goals. This kind of information is often not evident in the results of large-scale assessments. As I explained in Chapter 1, most large-scale assessments are norm-referenced—that is, they are designed primarily to rank students in comparison to each other, not to demonstrate how students meet specified criteria. Questions are purposefully placed on such tests to discriminate among students' performance so that results will fall out on a bell curve—only a few students will do really well, a few will do poorly, the bulk of the students will perform in the mid-range, with "grade level" designated as the average score. Because norm-referenced tests set the "standard" as the "average" score, it is technically impossible for all to meet the standard, and thus inevitable that half of all students will fail (Darling-Hammond 1994b; Darling-Hammond and Falk, 1997b; Oakes 1985).

There are, however, other ways to design assessments of students' learning that avoid these kinds of problems. These new kinds of assessments examine what students know and can do in ways that reveal what they understand, how they understand it, and the strategies that they use. Even large-scale tests intended to provide information about how students perform in relation to each other can provide this type of information. Such tests emphasize student performance in relation to publicly articulated standards that have been commonly agreed upon by communities (Darling-Hammond 1991, 1997; Darling-Hammond and Falk 1997a; Darling-Hammond and Wise 1985; Falk and Ort 1998; Herman, Aschbacher, and Winters 1992; New York State Curriculum and Assessment Council 1994; Resnick 1995). Much like the driver's license example mentioned earlier, these kinds of tests provide clear indicators of what students are expected to know so that they can work to meet the articulated expectations. "Grade level" or a passing mark on such tests is determined not by the average score of test takers, but by the degree to which a student meets the specified criteria. When tests are designed in such a way, it becomes technically possible (unlike in norm-referenced tests) for *all* students to achieve the desired standards and to perform "on grade level." While standards-referenced tests include items that reflect a range of difficulty levels, if the information and skills that appear on the tests are appropriate for the grade level and have been taught well by teachers, students should be able to master them.

Demonstrate Learning Progress with Multiple Forms of Evidence

Because learning is such a complex and variegated process, relying on any one form of evidence to evaluate students' proficiencies and progress offers, at best, a limited view—and sometimes even distorts the picture—of what students actually know and can do. Multiple forms of evidence provide a more accurate picture of students' abilities.

Some interesting insights about the benefits of using multiple forms of evidence to assess student progress are offered in a study that compares teachers' judgments of students' reading abilities derived from a variety of classroom-based assessments with the scores these same students achieved on one standardized reading test (Price, Schwabacher, and Chittenden 1993). The test that is analyzed in the study utilizes a cloze format, asking students to read a series of passages of increasing difficulty in which words have been omitted throughout. Students are asked to fill in the blanks by selecting the "correct" word from the multiple-choice answer form. Students' reading abilities are evaluated by analyzing the number of their correct answers in relation to the increasing length and complexity of the text. This evaluation is translated into a Degree of Reading Power (DRP) score. Students who read passages with short words and uncomplicated sentences get lower DRP ratings than those who read passages with lengthier words and more complicated sentences.

Although this formula for measuring reading ability is tidy, it does not adequately reflect the complexities involved in comprehending what is read. Very different kinds of texts can have the exact same DRP rating. For example, the popular children's book *Blueberries for Sal* (McCloskey 1950) has the same DRP rating as Hemingway's *Old Man and the Sea* (1952), an adult book that, despite its short length and easy-to-read words, reflects deeply on the meaning of life. Clearly, the DRP way of measuring reading leaves out important information, especially the degree to which a test taker can analyze, evaluate, or critically respond to a text.

The teachers in the study confirmed this point. They were asked to maintain a list of texts that they could verify their students had read and understood, look up the DRP rating for these texts, and then compare the rating of the texts with the scores the students achieved on the DRP test. Only 50 percent of students had test scores that were similar to the ratings of the books they had read. Of the students whose test scores did not correlate with what they had actually read, correlations were off the most for low-scoring students who were often reading texts that were rated some twenty or more points higher than their test scores indicated!

Such a discrepancy raises serious questions about the validity of this and similar kinds of assessment. It is also troubling because of the consequences associated with low test scores. Because test scores are used to rank schools and to make important decisions about students' lives, relying solely on this one form of evidence for evaluating reading can be misleading and sometimes harmful (Allington and McGill-Franzen 1992; Darling-Hammond and Falk 1997b; McGill-Franzen and Allington 1993).

Reveal the Impact of Instruction over Time

Not only is gathering different kinds of evidence of learning helpful to compile a picture of student progress, but also gathering this evidence over time helps to ensure that the picture is accurate. Assessments that provide an indication of how students have progressed over time offer a clearer and more valid picture of achievement than those that focus only on outcomes without regard to students' starting points. Because students and groups of students may vary greatly in their levels of performance—due to differences in family backgrounds, physiological makeup, and/or language proficiencies—assessment scores, to be most helpful, should indicate who started where and how far each has traveled in the journey toward proficiency. Measuring student progress in this way will furnish a fairer picture of achievement than scores that simply provide information about how students compare to a national norm.

Think of how this approach would have helped to assess Akeem, my struggling student described in Chapter 1. While his actual performance was not yet at the level of most students his age, in relation to where he began his progress throughout the year was tremendous. Yet the tests he took gave no indication of where he had come from, the progress he had made, what he actually was able to do. His scores were discouraging not only to him, but to his teachers as well. They gave the impression that no growth had taken place. If Akeem had been given an assessment that revealed and recognized the "value added" from his educational experiences, both he and his teachers would have been more rightly credited for the results of their efforts. Assessments that take into account students' growth over time do not penalize struggling students who have histories of low performance on tests or those teachers who choose to work with them (Chittenden and Courtney 1989; Falk and Darling-Hammond 1993; Falk, MacMurdy and Darling-Hammond 1995).

The characteristics discussed above can be found in many different types of assessments. Use the set of questions in Figure 2–1 to help you determine the degree to which the assessments you use embody these characteristics.

Consider Performance-Based Formats

Generally all the assessments that meet the criteria in Figure 2–1 utilize formats that look directly at student work (see Figure 2–2). These assessments examine evidence of students' learning through documented observations of students in the classroom, samples of students' written essays, drawings, or answers to problems, presentations or exhibitions of students' projects, videos of students in different

Qualities of Assessments in the Service of Learning

Do the assessment tasks mirror real-world work? Do they involve students in actually doing what people in the field do—writing, conducting experiments, doing research, designing products, and so on?

Is the information useful for instruction? Are students asked to justify answers or choices so that the process as well as the product of learning is revealed?

Is evidence about many dimensions and kinds of learning provided? Are diverse ways of learning and performing recognized?

Are tasks meaningful and worthy of doing? Do they emphasize in-depth understanding, higher-order thinking, problem-solving, and performance?

Are students assessed in relation to articulated criteria important for actual performance in that field?

Are differences in cultural and linguistic perspectives appreciated?

Are current understandings of learning and important aspects of the disciplines reflected? Is there support for learning experiences that draw connections between students' experiences and curriculum content?

Are key elements of the curriculum covered?

Can *accurate generalizations* be made about students' proficiencies based on the assessment results? Are *results reliable* across raters and consistent in meaning across locales?

Can the assessment be operationalized? Is the information it provides worth its cost and time?

Have opportunities to learn what is being assessed been provided?

Do positive consequences for learning result from the assessment's use?

Figure 2–1   ©2000 by Beverly Falk from *The Heart of the Matter*, Portsmouth, NH: Heinemann

Formats for Performance Assessments

written essays
projects
experiments
exhibitions
performances
collections of students' work

Figure 2–2   ©2000 by Beverly Falk from *The Heart of the Matter*, Portsmouth, NH: Heinemann

Comparing Different Kinds of Assessments

	INQUIRY ASSESSMENTS	EVALUATION ASSESSMENTS	
		Standards-Based	Norm-Referenced
PURPOSE	Designed to answer the questions: • What do students know? • What can they do? • How do they know/do what they know/do? • What are their strengths, dispositions, vulnerabilities?	Designed to answer the questions: In relation to a set of standards, • Do students know X? • Can students do X?	Designed to answer the questions: In relation to what other students know/can do, • Do students know X? • Can students do X?

FORMAT	Teachers' documentation:
	  Observations
	  Checklists
	Students' work:
	  Performances
	  Projects/experiments
	  Reports
	  Portfolios
	  Self-assessments
	Group processes:
	  Descriptive review of child
	  Looking at student work
		Teachers' documentation:
		  Observations
		  Checklists
		Students' work:
		  Performances
		  Projects/experiments
		  Reports
		  Portfolios
		  Self-assessments
		Group processes:
		  Looking at student work
		Tests:
		  Multiple-choice
		  Short answer
		  Extended response
		  Performance tasks
			Tests:
			Multiple-choice
			Short answer
			Extended response

MOST USEFUL FOR	• Informing instruction • Revealing information about students that can be shared with them and their parents	• Informing instruction • Revealing information about students that can be shared with them and their parents • Reporting to public	• Reporting to public and parents how students' performances compare to others

©2000 by Beverly Falk from *The Heart of the Matter*, Portsmouth, NH: Heinemann

Figure 2–3

situations, students' own reflections on their growth, and even the reflections of those who are most connected to the students' learning lives—family members, teachers, and other adults or peers.

Different Assessment Types Serve Different Purposes

It is important to understand that different types of assessments are designed to fulfill primarily different purposes—some to reveal information about students' strengths, interests, and unique ways of learning; some to offer evidence of achieving proficiency in a skill or content area as a result of a specific instructional experience; some to shed light on individual and group progress in order to address public questions about accountability. These different purposes require assessment forms that possess unique qualities and characteristics (Herman, Aschbacher, and Winters 1992). They generally fall into two approaches (see Figure 2–3). The first one, an inquiry approach, is designed to answer a broad question: "What can I learn about this student?" The second is a more evaluative approach, designed to answer a more specific question: "Can this student do _____?" Both types of assessments can answer their respective questions with information that is useful to teaching. In Chapters 3 and 4, I will examine more in depth the qualities of these two types of assessments.

Chapter 3

Keeping Track of Student Learning

Inquiry Assessments

Inquiry assessments look at students and their work in an open-ended way to find out what they know, how they know it, and what their strengths and vulnerabilities are. Inquiry assessments chronicle students' growth and development through a wide range of lenses or perspectives. This approach to assessment is almost always performance-based, relying on multiple forms of direct evidence of learning that are collected in a variety of meaningful, real-life contexts over an extended period of time.

Inquiry assessments aim to reveal a wider range of information about students than those demonstrated by most tests. In addition to showcasing students' accomplishments, they tap into complexities of subject matter that are difficult to reveal through conventional testing methods. They explore complexities of thinking that go beyond simply getting the "right answer": students' strategies and approaches to learning as well as the strengths they rely on (Kamii 1985, 1989; NAEYC 1991; NASBE 1988; NCTM 1989).

Through such formats as teacher-kept observations, student-kept records, actual samples of student work, and input from students and their families, inquiry assessments develop a unique portrait of each child's learning. This accumulated information can help teachers plan appropriate learning experiences and develop curriculum responsive to individual students' needs.

Context plays a major role in inquiry assessments. In addition to being highly sensitive to and reflective of the nuances of each learner, they are equally sensitive to differences in classroom environments, local resources, and/or teachers' judgments. Because these special qualities are difficult to measure quantitatively and difficult to compare from one student to another, inquiry assessments do not generally provide information that can be used to compare people across large groups. The emphasis is on individuals' growth in relation to themselves rather than in relation to others.

Using Inquiry Assessments in the Classroom

Inquiry assessments are most commonly used in the classroom. Many teachers collect evidence of students' work in various disciplines at regular intervals over the course of the school year. This kind of information documents the growth and development of each student over time. It is useful for informing students, their families, and successive teachers about what students have learned and what they can do, as well as what the particular strategies, strengths, styles, and interests are that students bring with them to their learning experiences.

Formats that document this kind of information are teacher-kept records, samples of student work, student-kept records, and other types of evidence about progress of groups of children. These provide teachers with occasions for reflection, learning, and communication that can influence their curriculum, instruction, and professional growth.

Teacher-Kept Records

Teacher-kept records can include documented observations of students, inventories or checklists of students' skill development, or notes from teacher-student conferences. Dated and entered into students' records, teacher-kept records can be used to track students' developing understandings and skills and to inform teachers' summary judgments for end-of-year or semester reports.

Just as students learn in different ways, teachers also observe and record students' progress in a multitude of ways. Some methods I have observed from teachers I have worked with are: jotting down observations on note cards; using sticky notes that get pasted into a notebook at the end of the day; and carrying a notebook that has sections demarcated for each child in which quick notes can be entered during the course of the day and longer reflections noted during preparation periods, lunches, or after-school hours.

Some teachers keep their records by regularly jotting down general comments about students' attitudes, ideas, and approaches to learning. Some teachers focus specifically on recording students' progress in relation to specific skills or content. Whatever the focus, when this is done regularly over time, information is compiled that, by the end of the school year, provides a substantial record of each student's growth. Descriptive, rather than evaluative language, is an important feature of this kind of assessment. In contrast to evaluative language, which frequently focuses on the end product of learning and heavily bears the judgment of the observer, descriptive language focuses on *how* something happens, noting the process as well as the product. Descriptive language holds the judgment of the observer in abeyance, focusing instead on unpacking the details of *why* one might be led to make a particular evaluation of a particular student in a particular context at a particular time. The descriptions below illustrate the difference. Compare these statements about Stephen's progress found in this report card:

> Stephen has an excellent vocabulary.
> Stephen does outstanding work.
> Stephen has excellent math skills.

with this version that was completed by his teacher after practicing her observation and documentation skills:

> Stephen uses a rich variety of descriptive words in his writing.
> Stephen works independently and intensely. He thinks critically, takes risks in putting forward new ideas, and is thorough in attention to details of presentation.
> Stephen is fluid in his thinking about number concepts. He can generally find several solutions to a problem and is able to explain them to others in a clear way.

This kind of feedback explains what makes Stephen's vocabulary and math skills "excellent," what about his work warrants the characterization of "outstanding." It provides Stephen's teachers, as well as his parents and himself, with a better understanding of *how* he does what he does.

When descriptions in this vein accumulate, they paint a picture of each student as a learner. This picture helps students, their families, and other teachers to recognize the students' strengths so that they can be built on further and so that areas in need of support can be identified in order to make plans for how to address them. Reading teacher Karen Kahn explains how this approach to assessment enabled her to be more responsive to her student Roberto and to communicate more effectively with his family (Falk 1994):

> The documentation that I kept of my work with Roberto showed the ways he grew as a reader that were not evident from his scores on the reading tests. He was a third grader who was not yet fluent in his reading and he got overwhelmed by all those long, boring, complicated paragraphs on the city/state reading test. As a result he received a very low score. The reading records I had regularly kept on him, however, demonstrated the changes he had made over the year and showed how much he actually could do. They documented how he was recognizing more words, how his miscues [mistakes, errors] were becoming increasingly related to

the meaning of the text, how he was correcting himself more frequently, and how he was reading longer, more complicated passages. This reassured me, as well as Roberto and his family, about his progress and gave me concrete suggestions for how they could support his reading at home.

When teachers first begin to document the work of their students in these ways, many of them feel overwhelmed by what seems like the enormity of the task. They often complain that such record keeping takes too much time and that it would be much easier and less time-consuming to keep track of this information in their memories. However, through their experiences of writing down their observations—from a variety of settings in a variety of ways—most recognize that they are learning more about their students from this process than they had ever imagined they could. They also begin to recognize that they are seeing things they had not noticed before. They soon get hooked on the process of collecting evidence and become advocates of keeping written records. They realize that memory of the details and the nuance that makes each child visible does indeed escape them in the blur of time passed; that only by collecting evidence about their students can they achieve a perspective of each student's unique growth over time. Jotting down and reflecting thus becomes part of the "teacherly" way of life. In much the same way that a researcher gathers evidence to better understand what it is she is studying, teachers too assume the researcher stance. They adopt an evidence-based approach to their teaching that informs instructional decisions for each individual.

Primary grade teacher Liz Edelstein sees herself as an educational researcher. She notes how keeping track of growth over time in the natural learning context helps her to better understand her students and to use this information in her instruction (Falk and Darling-Hammond 1993).

> Without the written record over time I would miss some kids. Only by looking back over records can you can start to see patterns in what the child is doing—reading, writing, and how it is all connected. All these bits of information come together into a picture that is particularly useful, especially for kids who are struggling in one way or another. My systematic documentation of children's learning has taught me that whatever conclusions I come to about a child or whatever I am going to try to do next has to be grounded in an observation or a piece of work. Observing children closely generally gives me a lot more than a specific recommendation or a particular method or thing to do for a kid. I walk away with some learning that I can apply to all kids.

Lucy Lopez, a bilingual special education teacher, has also found observing and recording to be helpful in her work with seven-year-old Miguel. Miguel was referred to Lucy's classroom after being diagnosed as "learning disabled" with attention deficit disorder. Her early impressions of him were:

> He used to jump all over and never focus in. He could never remember what he had learned. He didn't listen and it used to make me mad. (Falk, MacMurdy, and Darling-Hammond 1995)

Official school records for Miguel provided Lucy with little information about him that she could use in her teaching or that helped her cope with his behavior. They noted only what Miguel could *not* do. They focused only on how he performed isolated skills, with no mention of the strategies, approaches, or learning modalities that he employed as a learner. Here is an excerpt from Miguel's record that Lucy received when he entered her class:

> *Academic*
> Miguel does not demonstrate strong word-attack skills.
> Miguel does not read multisyllabic words.
> Miguel does not recognize content-related vocabulary.
> Miguel does not identify and use signal (key) words to increase understanding of a reading selection.
> Miguel does not read for a definite purpose: to obtain answers, to obtain general ideas of content, and for enjoyment.
> Miguel does not identify the main idea of a passage.
> Miguel does not use context clues to define unfamiliar words.
> Miguel does not spell words at grade level.
> Miguel does not write complete simple sentences.
>
> *Speech/Language and Hearing*
> Miguel is not able to use copular and auxiliary verb forms.

When Lucy first received Miguel's records she noticed that the phrase *Miguel does not* was used in almost every sentence. She was not surprised, therefore, that after presenting Miguel in the light of such deficits, the description of him concluded with the following:

> *Social Emotional Description*
> Miguel has a negative self-concept.

Frustrated by the lack of information about what Miguel actually *could* do, Lucy observed him for a while, systematically keeping track of his progress. As the weeks went by, she kept detailed notes of his learning strategies and the specific competencies he was mastering in reading and writing. She looked hard to find areas in which he demonstrated strength. This helped her to begin to see him differently. She began to see aspects of Miguel's learning that were formerly unnoticed—what Miguel *could* do, as opposed to only what he was *not* able to do.

Here is an entry from Lucy's notebook:

Miguel enjoys looking at books, especially books about animals, and can retell most stories that have been read to him. He memorized most of his favorite nursery rhymes with intonation and sang some of them. When reading he points to each word as he reads. He runs his fingers across the page when reading unfamiliar texts and uses picture clues to read unknown words. His sight vocabulary is developing through the use of "key words" [a personal word bank developed from the child's own interests].

This description of Miguel's reading reveals that, despite his lack of fluency in English and his inability to decode precisely, he is able to comprehend much of what he reads. Among Miguel's skills that are noted in the observations are his understanding that print goes from left to right, his recognition that a word is a word, his awareness of phonemes as evidenced in rhymes, his growing bank of automatically recognized high-frequency words, and the ways he uses context clues to help him figure out unknown words. The observation also reveals information about Miguel's interest in animals.

Lucy used this information to plan next steps for her instruction. She decided to find more books about animals that she could share with Miguel to further ignite his interests. She planned to continue to expose him to more and more words to increase his bank of sight words. And she launched explicit instruction about sound/symbol relationships so that he would have more tools available to him as he tried to decipher unfamiliar texts.

A later recorded observation of Miguel notes how Lucy's instructional planning worked:

Miguel is developing interest in written expression in English. He enjoys writing on a variety of topics. He draws illustrations to go with his writing. At times he uses phonetic spelling and is beginning to use sound/symbol relationships to spell unknown words. He easily recognizes many more words and uses them in his writing. He refers to his word bank when he is writing, looking around the classroom for the conventional spelling or asking a classmate for the correct spelling.

In these ways, observing and recording helped Lucy to see beyond the problems presented by Miguel's behavior; to see that he was indeed making progress as a learner. As she took further note of Miguel's strengths across other areas of the curriculum, she became more able to plan instruction that built on his interests and that met his specific learning needs. The following recommendations found in Lucy's notes demonstrate how she used the information she collected through her note-taking to lay the groundwork for her future teaching:

> Provide him with appropriately leveled texts around themes that will capture his interest.
>
> Build on developing phonetic skills through explicit instruction of middle vowel sounds, blends, etc.
>
> Make copies of appropriate books in both Spanish and English for Miguel to take home to read to his mother.
>
> Support Miguel's interest in developing a sight vocabulary by encouraging his collection of personally meaningful "key words" that can become both spelling and reading resources.
>
> Encourage Miguel's social interest in writing by supporting his efforts to use his classmates as learning resources and supports.
>
> Provide opportunities for involvement in projects, presentations, and class plays to foster Miguel's spoken language development.

These suggestions were passed on to Miguel's next teacher, making it possible to provide continuity in the school's approach to his instruction.

In addition to helping us think about students' progress systematically, documented observations also help to broaden our overall conceptions of what constitutes different students' "intelligence." The more we observe, the more sensitized we become to the diversity of talents and abilities in our students. This enables us to recognize students' abilities that formerly may not have been readily apparent. We are helped to recognize and appreciate what Howard Gardner refers to as *multiple intelligences*—linguistic, musical, bodily, spatial, and social strengths in addition to the logical and numerical ones emphasized most often in schools (Gardner 1983).

Noting and appreciating students' differences leads us to think about curriculum and teaching in a different way. We move away from standardized teaching approaches that require everyone to do the same thing in the same way. Instead we come to understand that no uniform teaching strategy or curriculum recipe is equally effective for all students. We move toward a differentiated instruction—one that provides different kinds of learners with different pathways to achieve mastery of important common concepts and skills.

Teachers everywhere, over the last decade, have been developing varieties of ways to keep track of their students' progress. Many formats and processes to assist in observing and recording learning are now commercially available. Among the most comprehensive of these for younger students are the Primary Language/ Learning Record (Barrs et al. 1988), and the Work Sampling System (Meisels et al. 1993). Both are frameworks for teachers to organize and synthesize information in order to look at an individual's growth over time.

Student Work Samples

Student work samples are another source of information that can provide important insights about students and their learning. These are frequently collected by teachers for a variety of purposes: to demonstrate each student's "best work," to document how students fulfill requirements that are mandated by the school or district, or to chronicle the growth and development of students' learning in an open-ended way. Later chapters discuss how student work collections can be used to demonstrate how students meet specified expectations. This section focuses on how student work can be used to inquire about the nature of a student's learning.

Inquiry collections of student work gather samples of what students do in a range of media from all discipline areas. The purpose is much the same as the purpose that drives the process of documenting observations—to gather evidence that chronicles progress, uncovers the nuances of how students approach learning, and reveals students' strengths and recurring interests. For example, writing samples reveal much about the nature of individuals' literacy development while math journals demonstrate—through algorithms as well as narratives—how students' mathematical thinking is progressing. Research reports, science experiments, projects, drawings, and paintings or other records of artistic endeavors provide information about learning as it is applied to solve problems that cut across disciplines. Photos of three-dimensional work (block buildings, woodworking, experiments, cooking, constructions) and photos of students engaged in activities with others (reading, tending to animals, sports, music, or dramatic play) give a sense of each student's interests and learning styles. Dating these items as they are archived gives a sense of students' progress over time.

The samples that follow were collected by teacher Mark Bushwinka to document the emergence of literacy in his first-grade student Carla (Falk and Darling-Hammond 1993). Together they provide a picture of Carla's progress over the course of the school year.

The first thing that Mark saved in the early months of school was a piece of Carla's writing that appeared as "scribbles" with accompanying stick figures (see

Figure 3–1. Carla's scribbles

Figure 3–1). His comments attached to this piece noted the undeveloped nature of Carla's figure drawings as well as her ability to differentiate between what she considered the print and the pictures.

Another of Carla's work samples that Mark saved from early on in the school year is a backward stencil of the alphabet (see Figure 3–2). Mark decided to save this piece because, to him, it indicated that Carla did not yet fully understand the concept of directionality—that English language print moves from left to right. He noted on the back of the paper that Carla "read" the alphabet to him from right to left.

Several months later Mark saved a page of words—*cat, frog, teddy bear, inkpad, stamps, markers and crayons*—that Carla had copied from classroom charts and labels (see Figure 3–3). This indicated to him that she was developing a vocabulary of frequently used words and that she was aware of the uses of print in her environment.

And finally, a writing sample Mark collected in the spring gives evidence of

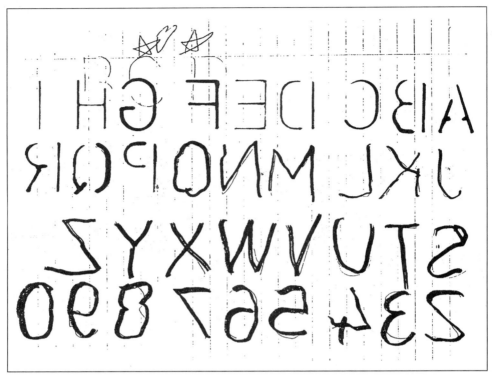

Figure 3–2.   Carla's backward stencil

the progress Carla has made. Her pictures are now detailed and include backgrounds for the people (see Figure 3–4). Her writing, which explains what the picture is about, has progressed to a mix of conventional words along with some phonetic spelling.

By systematically collecting these samples of work, Mark compiled a portrait of Carla that recorded her developing skills and understandings. Combined with documented observations that he had kept of Carla at work in the classroom, these helped him to note what Carla could do, what she understood, what her interests were, and what skills and understandings he needed to work on with her to enhance her future learning. He shared this information with Carla's family at parent-teacher conferences to help them understand her development.

In much the same way that the mementos in a scrapbook or family album

Figure 3–3.   Carla's page of words

chronicle important lifetime events, collections of student work provide a record of the evolution of students' developing insights, understandings, skills, and feelings. The samples of Carla's writing that are shared here reveal important insights about her literacy learning. Samples of her work in other discipline areas would indicate progress in these disciplines as well.

All of us can use this type of information to inform our teaching, to enhance our reports on students' progress, and to make communication with our students and their families more understandable and down-to-earth. Some schools use such collections of student work as the basis of home-school conferences. The school that I used to direct saved student work in portfolios that got passed on from teacher to teacher, grade to grade. We used to organize our home-school conferences around them, including the students in the conference to present and

Figure 3–4.   Carla's spring writing sample

reflect on their work. We would save common key items for our school records, sending the rest home at the end of each year for families to keep.

Student-Kept Records

Student-kept records are another helpful way to keep track of student learning. Even children of the youngest ages can keep records of their reading and writing, their projects, as well as their reflections on their work. These ongoing records can serve as an organizer for the activities of the classroom, making it possible for teachers to move away from whole group instruction as the only way of knowing what everybody is doing and enabling them, instead, to offer opportunities for independent and group work. By asking students to articulate and keep track of what they have done and what they think, students become more aware of their learning. They also develop a sense of responsibility, control, and ownership of their work.

Many classrooms have students keep logs of their reading. Ranging in format from lists kept in notebooks, on oak tag bookmarks, or on teacher-designed forms (see Figure 3–5), reading logs provide a way for students to keep track of what they have read, when they read it, and what they thought about what they read. This information provides the teacher with a sense of the range of genres and difficulty level of texts that the students are able to read. It also provides a means for students to work independently and to keep track of their learning so that they and their teachers get a sense of the continuity in their work.

Student-kept records can be used for other subjects as well. Math journals or notebooks, for example, can be used to document what students can do and what they understand about important concepts and skills. Students use such journals to do daily math assignments, to record their own invented problems, or to work on teacher-designed individualized problems.

Some of the teachers I know use math journals to record how students solve "problems of the week." Problems of the week—usually three or four—are assigned

READING LOG FOR _____

DATE	BOOK - TITLE, AUTHOR	WHO READ IT	COMMENTS

Figure 3–5.   Reading Log

at the beginning of the week but not discussed until the end. They are usually word problems that involve multiple steps and that require thought, time, and the ability to apply an array of skills and understandings. Because the problems often have more than one right answer, students need to do more than solve them; they must explain what they did to solve them. This sharing of thinking and different strategies can be done at a class meeting. The math journals serve as a record *of* students' understandings as well as a vehicle by which students are guided to work *for* understanding.

In a similar way, project folders can be used to chronicle students' understandings in a variety of disciplines. Because projects offer the opportunity for students to apply valued knowledge and skills, project work that is done in the course of classroom life can be a valuable learning experience in addition to being a demonstration of that learning. Teachers can use project folders to keep track of what students do during classroom time allocated for project work—the questions that arose, how they proceeded to answer those questions, and what they learned as a result. Examining project folders that are used in this way should provide understandings about what students know and what they can do that are useful in planning next steps for learning in a manner that is responsive to students' understandings and needs.

Providing time for students to share their work records with their classmates can also be valuable. The discussions that can ensue from this type of sharing help students to clarify their thinking. In addition, such conversations can stimulate new directions that can deepen and extend individual or group work. Take, for example, my colleague Susan Gordon's fifth-grade class' study of flight (Falk 1993). Initiated by a trip to an aeronautics museum, the flight curriculum engaged students in literacy, math, science, and social studies activities. For this study, all students were required to complete a common set of activities. In addition, each student was challenged to pursue one aspect of the study independently and in-depth. Some created airplane designs and then built models of them. Some did research on aviation history. Some read the biographies of famous pilots. At regular intervals Susan led the class in a discussion of their project work, inviting different students to share the progress of their projects with the other students in the class. This inevitably led to new questions for the presenters, raised by others in the class, that provided directions for further study.

For example, when Howard shared what he was learning about how the design of planes had changed over time, someone asked him, "Why did some of the early two-seater planes have the pilot sit in a backseat?" To answer this question he revisited his history references to fill in the details that he did not know. Or when E'Shante shared what he was learning about aerodynamics from the paper air vehicles that he was making, he was asked, "How does a helicopter go forward?" This question led him to experiment more with making paper helicopters so that he could answer that question.

The ongoing assessment records of work kept by Susan's class and subsequently shared at their class meetings made it possible for the whole group to develop a common body of knowledge without everyone having to do the same thing at the same time. Group discussions of works-in-progress provided each individual with guidance for their studies as well exposure to a wider world of information and ideas than any one individual could get from pursuing a study alone.

Group learning in Susan's classroom was further enhanced by recording what took place in class discussions and activities. Documented on large chart paper and displayed sequentially on classroom walls, a chronicle of the classroom as a learning community was created for all members to use as a reference and reminder over time. The Reggio Emilia schools in northern Italy have publicized this way of documenting the learning journey of a whole class. Recording class learning in this way enables discussion to elevate to deeper discourse, group remembering to support revisiting of powerful ideas, symbols to turn into languages of learning, listening to include hearing others' meanings, understanding to lead to provocation of new ideas, encounters to expand into projects, community involvement to develop into partnerships, and assessment to become rich inquiry (Edwards, Gandini, and Forman 1998).

Using Group Inquiry Assessment Processes

Some school communities engage in inquiry-oriented assessment processes that help them learn together about individual students—their strategies, strengths, interests, or dispositions. The Child Study, a mainstay of early childhood educational practice, is the embodiment of this assessment approach (Cohen et al. 1993). Other powerful derivatives are the Collaborative Assessment Conference (Seidel 1998) and the Descriptive Review Process (Prospect Center 1986).

All of these approaches are formal, collaborative (sometimes involving whole faculties), descriptive processes for addressing an issue, question, or concern about a student in order to better support her learning. A presenter describes a child and/or her work as fully and in as balanced a way as possible. The perspectives through which the child or her work is described are multiple. Samples of work are presented to illustrate questions or issues that need to be explored. The intent of these processes is to gain access to the child's modes of thinking and learning and to see her world from her own point of view: What catches her attention? What arouses her wonder and curiosity? What sustains her interest and purpose for learning?

Figure 3–6 is one protocol for teachers to look together at student work.

1. What was the context in which the work was created?
2. What questions does this work raise about the student—the student's intent, interests?
3. What does this work tell us about what the student understands, what the student can do, and how the student meets standards/expectations for the work?
4. What does this work demonstrate about the student's growth over time?
5. What does this work tell us about the instruction and learning environment that prompted the work? How effective were the assignment and teaching strategies?
6. What does this work suggest about the kind of teaching and opportunities for learning that should come next for this student?

Figure 3–6. Guiding Questions for Looking Together at Student Work

Teachers I know who have used these questions have found them to enhance their understandings of their children's learning.

Another group process for learning about students is the Descriptive Review Process (Prospect Center 1986). It studies individuals by describing them through a variety of perspectives:

the child's physical presence and gesture
the child's disposition
the child's relationships with other children and adults
the child's activities and interests
the child's approach to formal learning
the child's strengths and vulnerabilities

In the Descriptive Review Process a presenter, usually the child's teacher, shares evidence about a particular child in order to better understand a specific issue or question. Prior to the presentation, an appointed chairperson and the presenter discuss and define one or more focusing questions that are central to gaining an understanding of the child. The chairperson also obtains background knowledge and a sense of the history of the child.

The chairperson shares this information in a brief opening presentation at the beginning of the review process. This opening presentation also includes a reminder to participants of the Descriptive Review Process code of conduct: no gossip, no innuendo, no judgmental language; and its focus: to find ways to support growth by building on the strengths of children. A note-taker is assigned to document the entire process for the school's and the child's records.

The presenter then describes the child through the perspectives listed above. The child's work is used to verify, validate, and illustrate points made during the presentation. After the presenter speaks, the chair gives an overview of what was said, highlighting themes and issues that emerged from the portrait of the child given by the presenter. Then other participants are invited, in a round-robin fashion—no cross-conversations allowed—to comment and reflect on what they have heard. When the round-robin is completed, the chair repeats back to the participants all that has been said and invites the presenter to respond. After the presenter responds to the first set of comments, review participants are invited to speak once again, this time to make suggestions about what changes in classroom environment or teaching practices might better address the needs of the child. The chair concludes with a summation of what has taken place, emphasizing any new perspectives on the child that have emerged and any new ideas for how to work with the child.

The Guiding Questions for Looking at Student Work and the Descriptive Review Process are structured formats that enable the people charged with supporting children's learning to use empirical information to assess growth and to use the assessment to support teaching. These processes are meant to engage participants in considering not how to better *fix* the child, but rather to reflect on what kind of supports and responses will best provide for the child's needs. The intent of both processes is to make fully visible the strengths and the unique attributes of each child. Doing this can be especially helpful in schools that seek to include *all* of the children whom they serve in the ranks of successful learners. A teacher who has engaged in such work speaks to the power of this approach (Falk 1994):

> The value of an education will never be missed by visible and included children. They will be too excited by their own wonderful ideas and strengths—pointed out to them by their teachers—to give up on their own learning. (Miller 1990, 35)

Weaving Assessment into the Curriculum: An Interactive Cycle

When all of the different modes of inquiry-oriented assessment—teacher observations, student work, student-kept records, and collaborative processes of looking at student work—are used in combination, they provide a fulsome picture of individuals' growth. Together they provide evidence that can inform and support teaching and learning. This evidence-based approach to teaching weaves assessment, curriculum, and instruction together (see Figure 3–7).

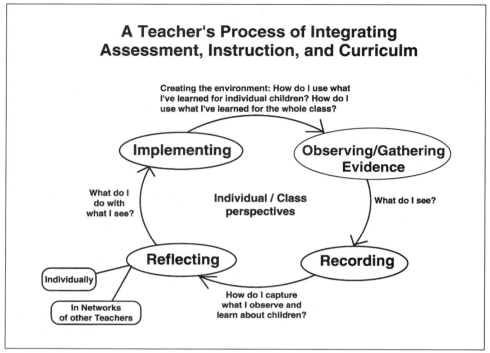

Figure 3–7   ©2000 by Beverly Falk from *The Heart of the Matter*, Portsmouth, NH: Heinemann

The process of systematically gathering evidence, reflecting on its meaning, and using it to shape our teaching strategies offers us understandings of our students that can be used to make instructional decisions responsive to the unique needs, interests, and understandings of each learner. An evidence-based approach to teaching helps us make teaching a more professional act. It moves us away from personal feelings or intuition as a guide to our actions toward a systematic process of using known facts to inform and support our instruction.

Chapter 4

Evaluation in a Different Key

Standards-Based Performance Assessments

Although inquiry assessments offer rich information about students and the quality of their learning, they generally do not have a place in assessment systems that evaluate student performance for accountability purposes. This is because most inquiry assessments used by teachers in their classrooms, while useful to instruction, do not focus on whether or not students have met common predetermined expectations. Inquiry assessments are generally idiosyncratic and nonstandardized and thus not suitable for making comparisons or for reporting progress of students across groups. Because teachers often differ in what they consider important to assess, the skills and knowledge they examine varies greatly from one classroom to another. And because, among teachers, there are generally not shared beliefs about the purposes, goals, and expectations of teaching or about what characterizes "quality" work, many teachers bring different interpretations to the evidence they collect and thus evaluate it quite differently. Add to these differences the wide array of instructional programs that teachers use, as well as the wide variation in teachers' skills and knowledge, and it is easy to see how problematic it could be to use inquiry assessments for reporting on student progress and for comparing it across groups.

Evaluating and Reporting Student Progress Across Groups: The Need for Standardization and the Dilemmas This Creates

It is to address these issues that standardized formats have come to be relied on for evaluating and reporting students' progress on a large scale. The reasoning goes something like this: By using standardized ways of examining the same skills and the same content, through the same format with the same criteria, in similar contexts at similar times, the likelihood will be increased that assessment results will mean the same thing in different places. It is also reasoned that the formats used in standardized tests (answers that are clearly right or wrong and that translate easily into a score) enable information about large numbers of students to be reported in a manageable and publicly accessible way.

But while this standardization does, indeed, make the information obtained from assessments easily reportable, it also makes the assessments limited in their ability to provide the kind of rich information about students that is useful for teaching and that benefits student learning. The need to standardize (so that, for example, what is considered to be "accomplished" work in one locale represents the same level of accomplishment in another) drives the test format toward a focus on what is easiest to measure, often at the expense of what is most important.

Most tests that we have known in our learning lives are examples of this phenomenon. They focus primarily on information that can be measured in *yes/no* and *right/wrong* answers. Relying heavily on one time, sit-down, paper and pencil formats to obtain evidence of what test takers know, they provide little information about whether the test taker can actually apply that knowledge in real-life contexts or whether the test taker understands what he is doing. Only the final answers matter; not how these answers are arrived at. Little insight is provided about the strategies test takers use or the strengths and interests that guide their learning.

These shortcomings of standardized tests pose real problems. But because we have no other ways to give us information about student progress across schools, we are forced to rely on existing tests that not only are of little use to our teaching, but that also do not reflect what many of us think matters most about our students' learning.

This is a dilemma we need to solve. Assessments powerfully drive instruction. Because of this, we need to find ways to assess student learning that reliably report on student progress and that are also useful and valid to our teaching. No matter their purpose, *all* assessments need to support teaching and learning.

We are faced with the challenge, then, of finding or creating assessments that are uniform enough to reveal and assess important goals in trustworthy ways—so that they can be used for reporting how students and schools are doing—but that also are context-embedded and flexible enough so that they are responsive to individual differences, represent real-world performance, and capture students' genuine abilities and understandings. We need assessments that validly reflect what we care about and are actually trying to measure (Linn 1987; Linn, Baker, and Dunbar, 1991; Moss 1994).

Accountability: Democracy's Social Contract with the Public

Why, some might ask, should we spend our energies and efforts trying to pursue this difficult task? Why can't teachers just keep track of students' learning in their own individual ways that they know are useful to instruction? Why do we have to worry about external accountability for student learning? Why can't we define accountability differently so that it relies on information that is more personal, more directly connected to context and different individuals' needs?

Any discussion about accountability must start from the fact that schools operate on the basis of an implicit "social contract" between the school and the community. Each one of us sends our children to school in good faith that the school will teach them to learn. In the case of public schools, the "social contract" is explicit. The government, by using our tax dollars to finance schools and by requiring each and every one of us to send our children to school for a minimum of ten to twelve years, assumes responsibility for providing an adequate education to every child. Mechanisms are needed to ensure and demonstrate that this promise is upheld. Regardless of the conditions in which students live, what background they come from, or what language they speak, the promise of public education is supposed to be that every child will be provided with access to what W. E. B. Du Bois called the "right to learn":

> Of all the civil rights for which the world has struggled and fought for 5,000 years, the right to learn is undoubtedly the most fundamental. . . . The freedom to learn . . . has been bought by bitter sacrifice. And whatever we may think of the curtailment of other civil rights, we should fight to the last ditch to keep open the right to learn, the right to have examined in our school not only what we believe, but what we do not believe; not only what our leaders say, but what the leaders of other groups and nations, and the leaders of other centuries have said. We must insist upon this to give our children the fairness of a start which will equip them with such an array of facts and such an attitude toward truth that they can have a real chance to judge what the world is and what its greater minds have thought it might be. (Dubois 1949, in Darling-Hammond 1997, 1)

It was, in part, in the context of this goal that standardized tests were developed in the first place. Our experiences with them over the last century, however, have led us to understand all too well the problems that these tests present. And our ever-deepening awareness and sensitivity to the unequal conditions experienced by the increasingly diverse population in our country has also led us to realize that providing the "right to learn" for all children requires far more than demanding common student outcomes on a series of standardized tests.

Yes, our government—states, communities, districts, schools, and those who work within them—needs to be accountable for the schooling we provide for the students of our nation. However, genuine responsibility for equal-quality schooling is not achieved by only administering tests. It involves paying attention to a host of factors that schools need in order to do their jobs well. If we are going to demand that all students achieve certain common expectations, then we also must ensure that all schools receive the ingredients needed to enable them to make this possible. We will not be able to make this happen without rectifying the unequal distribution of resources that affect the quality of services schools provide. Schools need adequate financing, properly maintained buildings, quality books, materials, and enrichment activities if they are to meet students' needs.

Also needed is attention to building the capacities of those charged with supporting students' learning. Attention must be paid to enhancing teachers' knowledge and skills through better teacher preparation programs, more effective professional development initiatives, teacher salaries that are competitive with other professions, and certification and licensing procedures that can guarantee quality teaching in all classrooms, schools, and districts. All of these factors are "opportunities to learn" that students need and that must be addressed if we are truly to provide all with the quality schooling that is their birth-given "right to learn."

Educational accountability, however, involves even more than these issues. Ultimately it has to do with issues far beyond the quality of schooling. It is related to the quality of other aspects of life as well—housing, health care, jobs, and food. Children who do not have access to these cannot be expected to learn. We cannot really talk of genuine accountability if we do not work on and address all of these issues.

While we work on these bigger challenges, the need still remains, however, for better assessments of student learning that can be used to provide some of the information the public needs and wants to know about how students progress within and across schools.

Standards: A Means to School Improvement and Accountability

This is where standards have entered into the national educational conversation. Standards have been posed as both a means to attain school improvement and, when connected to standards-based assessments, to provide information needed for accountability.

The birth of the standards movement can be traced to the 1983 report "A Nation at Risk." This report, prophesizing that our nation's economic well-being and military superiority is connected to our educational progress, warned that our educational system exemplified a "rising tide of mediocrity that threatens our very future as a Nation and as a people." (National Commission on Excellence in Education 1983, 5). Mobilized by this alert, then-President George H. Bush convened a special summit with the National Governor's Association in 1991 to address the educational preparedness of American youth. This group drafted a document, "The National Education Goals Report: Building a Nation of Learners," which delineated six broad goals for education. Two of the six goals related directly to academic achievement in the traditional disciplines:

> Goal 3: By the year 2000, American students will leave grades four, eight, and twelve having demonstrated competency in challenging subject matter including English, mathematics, science, history, and geography; and every school in America will ensure that all students learn to use their minds well so they may be prepared for responsible citizenship, further learning, and productive employment in our modern economy.
>
> Goal 4: By the year 2000, U.S. students will be first in the world in science and mathematics achievement. (National Education Goals Panel 1991, 4)

As a follow-up to the governors' summit, two groups—the National Education Goals Panel and the National Council on Education Standards and Testing—were established to devise content standards for each of the academic disciplines and to create assessments that would be matched to those standards. Even before this effort got underway, however, the National Council of Teachers of Mathematics (NCTM), the national professional organization for mathematics teachers, had already been working on and released a document that outlined standards for their field. This document, acclaimed for its clarity, its focus on essential topics and concepts, and its approach to teaching emphasizing understanding and the ability to apply mathematical knowledge rather than rote memorization and manipulation of algorithms, triggered a flurry of standards-making initiatives across the nation. National professional organizations representing the different disciplines simultaneously began to try to emulate what NCTM had done.

The standards movement got another major boost when the "Goals 2000: Educate America Act" passed in 1994. It called for every state to develop standards and new assessments that would evaluate how students were progressing toward them. Since that time, forty-nine states have established state-level academic standards for the children in their schools. Forty states have standards in all "core subjects" (Kappner 1999). These efforts coincided with a wave of standards-making efforts in the areas of teacher preparation, licensing, and certification, led first by professional organizations and then followed by states (Holmes Group 1986; National Commission on Teaching and America's Future 1996).

Much of the motivation for these initiatives stems from the belief that standards and standards-based assessments, by clearly articulating desired outcomes and by assessing whether those outcomes have been met, can be used to guide practice, to create a more coherent curriculum, and to ensure that all students are educated equally (American Federation of Teachers 1997; Marzano and Kendall 1996; Ravitch 1995).

Standards-Based Assessments: Bridging the Strengths of Inquiry and Evaluation Assessments

Assessments that are referenced to standards combine some of the features of inquiry assessments with some of the features of the evaluation tests that have traditionally been used for reporting student progress. Standards-based assessments are evaluative in that they measure if students know specific facts, possess certain skills, or have command of key concepts. However, they evaluate student learning in ways that are different from those employed by most traditional tests: They look at student learning in relation to standards that have been articulated for the discipline and age level and they evaluate this learning in performance-oriented ways that call on students to apply their knowledge and explain what they understand. Relying heavily on such formats as essays, multistep tasks, and extended responses, standards-based performance assessments also contain some of the features of inquiry assessments: They reveal important insights about the quality of students' understandings and approaches to learning and they both inform as well as influence instruction to utilize richer learning contexts in the classroom. Standards-based assessments thus incorporate the strengths of both inquiry assessments and evaluative tests. They show *what* students know as well as *how* they know it (see Figure 2-3, page 39).

Standards-based assessments, in and of themselves, do not necessarily support teaching and learning. The degree to which they do so is dependent on a complex set of factors that include the quality of the standards they are designed to assess and how the assessments are put to use. If the standards around which the tasks are developed include worthy goals—such as the ability to understand and apply knowledge, to think critically and creatively, to problem pose as well as problem solve—then the assessments, in order to provide evidence of how students are approaching these goals, will by necessity be performance-oriented and will provide opportunities for students to demonstrate what they know in a variety of ways. When standards and standards-based assessments are designed in these ways, they hold great potential for positively impacting teaching and learning.

If, however, the standards around which the assessments are built are merely repackaged lists of endless discrete facts—the hallmark of the teaching-as-telling approach to learning—then the assessments used to measure them will be less likely to support such worthy goals as learning for understanding and being able to apply these understandings. Standards conceived of in this way will offer few opportunities for individuals who think in different ways to learn and to express understandings of that learning. Assessments based on these kinds of standards will most likely be closed-ended tasks that do not utilize performance formats, that reveal little about test takers' approaches to learning, and that offer few opportunities for diverse learners to demonstrate what they know and can do.

When standards-based assessments are conceived around worthy goals, they usually possess several key features that differentiate them from other assessments designed to evaluate student learning (see Figure 4–1). Standards-based assessments are both explicit and public about the criteria for how students are to be evaluated. They outline, in advance, the qualities of work that are to be assessed. They do this in two ways: through scoring guides accompanying the assessments that describe what the qualities being assessed look like at varying degrees of proficiency—from beginning to accomplished; and by providing benchmark samples of student work that offer test takers (and teachers too) clear images of what work looks like at different proficiency levels.

The task shown in Figure 4–2, created as a pilot task for the newly developed

Features of Standards-Based Assessments

- Embody important learning goals (standards) in a task
- Utilize performance formats
- Clearly articulate criteria for how to do the task
- Outline the qualities that will be evaluated in the task
- Describe what the qualities that will be evaluated look like at different levels of proficiency in rubrics, scoring guides, or scales
- Provide models (benchmarks) of what work looks like at different levels of proficiency

Figure 4–1   ©2000 by Beverly Falk from *The Heart of the Matter*, Portsmouth, NH: Heinemann

Question and Rubric

Question 15:

15. The students in the 5th grade at the Elm Street School wanted to find out how many students in each grade attended summer camp. They took a survey and tallied the results shown in the table below.

Grade	Attended Camp
1	⊞ I
2	⊞ IIII
3	⊞ ⊞ III
4	⊞ ⊞ ⊞ IIII
5	⊞ ⊞ ⊞ ⊞ I

Use their data to construct a graph on the grid provided.

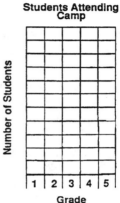

Write one or two sentences that tell what you learned from the graph.

RUBRIC

3 Points

Either correct graph, appropriately labeled, correct use of scale **OR** Existing graph extended correctly **AND** Logical written response

2 Points

Graph contains one error in transferring data or sacle **AND** Logical written response

1 Point

Correct graphs data from tally **BUT** Scale missing or incorrect Lacks logical written response **OR** Graph contains more than one minor error **BUT** Response is logical for graph as drawn

0 Points

Graph, scale and written response are inaccurate **OR** No response

Figure 4–2.   Fourth-Grade Math Task and Rubric

New York State Fourth Grade Mathematics Assessment, offers an example of these features of standards-based assessments.

Notice how the task calls for the test taker to solve problems by applying knowledge and by explaining how the answer was obtained. Notice how the criteria for satisfactory performance are explained *in advance* through a scoring rubric or guide describing the qualities that will be assessed and what they look like at differing levels of proficiency. Notice how task expectations are further clarified through the accompanying samples of student work that represent the different score levels, providing images of what the descriptions in the scoring guides look like (see Figure 4–3).

This clear articulation of expectations can be especially helpful to struggling students who have had little prior exposure to the skills and expectations that support school-based learning. Often this is due to the fact that they simply have not had the learning opportunities to which other students have been exposed.

Clarifying Goals and Expectations for Students

We all know that some children more than others come to school already equipped with the skills and behaviors that result in school success. They speak the same language as the school, have been read to thousands of times in the language of the school, have had countless opportunities to converse and to write in ways that are similar to what is done in school, and have been exposed to many different models of school achievement and success.

In contrast, some children have had little of these supports. They may come from a culture that has different "funds of knowledge"—experiences, strengths, and resources—than those that contribute to school success (Moll and Greenberg 1990). They may come from families who speak a different language, who cannot or do not have time to read to them, who cannot help them with their homework, or who have had little experience with doing a research report or essay. For these children, the clearly stated criteria of well-developed, standards-based assessments can make a world of difference in their ability to accomplish school-based expectations and to succeed in school-based work. Instead of gaining exposure to the desired standard of performance only *after the fact*—through critical responses from their teachers after their work has been handed in—standards-based performance assessments make the expectations, as well as images of accomplished work, clear in advance. In this way, standards-based performance assessments help to "level the playing field" a bit for students who have had vastly unequal opportunities, resources, and supports for their learning (Falk and Ort, 1998; Resnick 1994; Rothman 1997).

Anchor Papers

Question 15:

Grade 4

15. The students in the 5th grade at the Elm Street School wanted to find out how many students in each grade attended summer camp. They took a survey and tallied the results shown in the table below.

Grade	Attended Camp
1	卌 I
2	卌 IIII
3	卌 卌 III
4	卌 卌 卌 IIII
5	卌 卌 卌 卌 I

Use their data to construct a graph on the grid provided.

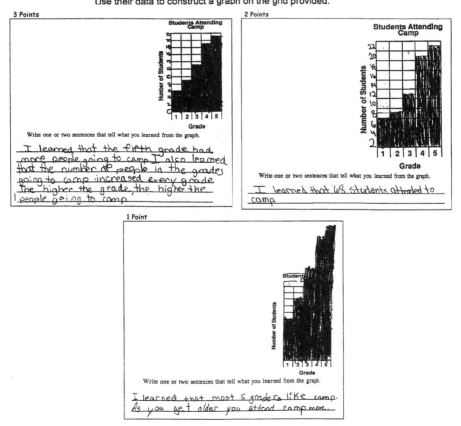

3 Points

Students Attending Camp

Number of Students

Grade 1 2 3 4 5

Write one or two sentences that tell what you learned from the graph.

I learned that the fifth grade had more people going to camp. I also learned that the number of people in the grades going to camp increased every grade. The higher the grade, the higher the people going to camp.

2 Points

Students Attending Camp

Number of Students

Grade 1 2 3 4 5

Write one or two sentences that tell what you learned from the graph.

I learned that 68 students attended to camp.

1 Point

Students

Number of Students

Grade 1 2 3 4 5

Write one or two sentences that tell what you learned from the graph.

I learned that most 5 graders like camp. As you get older you attend camp more.

Figure 4–3. Samples of Scored Fourth-Grade Math Tasks

Emphasizing Understanding and Application of Knowledge

Another feature of standards-based performance assessments that has the potential to be helpful to students is the performance-oriented formats that they use (Darling-Hammond and Falk 1997a). By calling on students to apply their knowledge in real-world situations and to actually demonstrate what they understand—in the form of written essays, projects, experiments, exhibitions, performances, or collections of students' work—standards-based performance assessments provide opportunities for students who have different learning styles and strengths to demonstrate their proficiencies in a variety of ways (Chittenden and Courtney 1989; Darling-Hammond, Ancess, and Falk 1995; Falk and Larson 1995; McDonald et al. 1993; Mitchell 1992; Perrone 1991).

Assessments that include some kind of performance are helpful to teachers as well as students. Performance tasks guide teachers to teach in ways that emphasize real-life application of knowledge. This should free teachers from the pressures of having to prepare students to do well on traditional tests. To prepare for performance assessments, teachers should not have to split their instructional time between teaching in real-life, context-rich ways and doing "test-prep" activities that teach students how to maneuver the "tricks" and the artificial multiple-choice formats found in many standardized tests. The best preparation for helping students to do well on performance assessments designed around worthy goals is for teachers to focus their full attention on fostering meaningful, in-depth, lifelike learning.

Guiding Teachers' Instruction

Standards-based performance assessments are helpful to teachers in still other ways. The tasks' clear expectations serve as a guide to instruction, reminding teachers about the critical issues and key competencies of the standards that they need to include in their teaching. In addition to making expectations explicit, standards-based assessments are helpful because they articulate expectations for outcomes rather than methods for instruction. Teachers do not have to teach in only one way to have students do well on these assessments. As long as teachers are preparing students to meet the standards, they are free to utilize a range of different instructional techniques and a variety of learning situations that are responsive to the varied learning modalities of their students.

Figure 4–4 is an example of a standards-based performance task and its rubric that illustrates these features of standards-based performance assessments. It is designed to assess a set of math, science, and technology standards. It gives students a chance to demonstrate what they know in a variety of ways by calling on students to work individually as well as in groups, to solve problems numerically as well as

Keep It Cool!

The Problem

Your class is planning an overnight camping trip. The students on the Food Committee have decided to use ice to keep the food cool. They need a storage container that will do the best possible job of keeping the ice from melting too quickly.

Your Task

Design and build a model of a container that can keep food cool by preventing ice from melting for 24 hours. The model container should keep 240 mL of water frozen for 24 hours. The size of your model may not exceed 2000 cubic centimeters. The shape of the container, the materials from which it is made and the insulation method are up to you to decide. Your job is to explore the many aspects of this problem and to offer well thought out, cost-effective solutions.

You are advised to develop a working journal in which you will keep ideas, drawings, experimental procedures and data. Your journal should serve as your reminder of important ideas and findings. Therefore, you should keep it clear and organized. One way to organize your journal is to use the same format as is used for the Scoring Sheet in this booklet.

Group Work
Possible Approaches To Solving the Problem
• Brainstorm and discuss the various factors that might affect the ability of a container to keep ice from melting.
• Brainstorm other factors that should be considered to make the container practical and appropriate for using it to keep food cool.
• Investigate this problem and collect needed information from experiments, textbooks, library sources, and other resources. Keep notes of your work and records of data collected.
• Design and conduct a series of investigatory studies to explore this topic.
• Draw sketches of several possible solutions. Have your teacher check your solutions for safety considerations.
• Share ideas with the rest of the students in the class.
• Make a choice from among the various possible solutions that your team investigated and explain the reasons for your group's choice.

Procedures to Use
• Produce a scale drawing of your chosen container design.
• Use the scale drawing to build your container.
• Place 240 mL of water in a container and freeze it. Put the ice into the container you designed, close it, and leave it at room temperature for 24 hours.
• Open the container, and observe and analyze the results.
• Based on your results, make recommendations for improving or redesigning your container. Explain and justify your recommendations.

Reporting Your Findings
Group Presentation
Prepare a multimedia presentation to describe your solution to the problem to the rest of your class. A multimedia presentation uses more than one mode to make the presentation clear and interesting to other students. (For example, you can add visuals to your oral presentation to show or clarify procedures used. Or, if you choose to be a high-tech presenter, you might use video clips, computer simulations and edited sound to augment your presentation.) Explain what your group did, where you got your information, what you learned, and what you would change if you did the project again.

Individual Work
Write a report to the chairperson of the camping trip Food Committee. The report should include the following:
• Description of your investigations.
• Assumptions that you made and the supporting data you used to design, build, and test your prototype product.
• Description and analysis of the model for your team's chosen solution.
• The changes you would make to your model so that it could actually be used to keep food cool by keeping ice from melting too quickly. Add any information that in your opinion will persuade the Food Committee to accept your idea.

Your individual report should not exceed four pages, including any graphs or charts.

Evaluation
As a class decide whether you want to be evaluated on a team presentation, or on an individual written report. Use the Scoring Sheet in your booklet to evaluate the quality of either your team's presentation or your individual written report. The team presentation or the individual written report should reflect all the Scored Dimensions on the Scoring Sheet.

Figure 4–4.   Keep It Cool! Task

through a model, and to explain understandings both in writing and through an oral presentation.

Balancing Tensions Between Standards and Standardization

While it is harder to standardize performance-based demonstrations of knowledge and skills than it is to standardize yes/no or fill in the blank questions, it *is* possible to do so without losing the richness and the usefulness of the information that the performance-based demonstration offers. Standards-based performance assessments can thus be designed to serve dual purposes—to evaluate student progress as well as to support teaching and learning. They can be designed to determine if students are meeting important learning goals, to ensure that what is being examined in one student or one classroom is comparable to what is being examined in another, *and* to provide insights about how students are approaching their learning. In this way, they have the potential to be useful for informing instruction in the classroom as well as for reporting progress outside of it. Teachers,

Student Name _____ Team Identity _____

4 = Excellent Performance   3 = Proficient Performance, Needs Minor Revisions
2 = Acceptable Performance, Needs Major Revisions   1 = Unacceptable Performance

Scored Dimension   **Level of Performance**

Scored Dimension	Score	Justification
SCIENTIFIC INQUIRY	**Score**	**Justification**
Student/Team Identified and thoroughly explored the effects of various factors related to the task.		
Clearly described scientific investigations in a way that would allow others to repeat them.		
Used data and scientific analysis to justify conclusions.		
MATHEMATICAL ANALYSIS	**Score**	**Justification**
Collected data and used mathematical operations (measuring, calculating, estimating, etc.) to find patterns and relationships.		
Presented data in an effective way using charts, graphs, tables, equations, etc.		
Used mathematical findings to help better understand and solve the problem..		
TECHNOLOGICAL DESIGN	**Score**	**Justification**
Sketched, drew, or made 3-D models of several alternative solutions.		
Made choices based upon the cost, availability, and suitability of materials.		
Tested the model and justified it according to the design criteria.		
Used tools, machines and materials safely and skillfully.		
TEAMWORK	**Score**	**Justification**
Performed the work in a responsible, logical, and organized way.		
Shared ideas with team members and classmates.		
COMMUNICATION	**Score**	**Justification**
Searched for and effectively integrated information from different sources.		
Presented the problem, procedures, data and solutions in a clear and organized way.		
Used media to raise interest and improve presentation.		

Figure 4–4.   (Continued)

schools, or districts can even aggregate the test results of standards-based performance assessments to determine what percentage of students achieved the desired goals at each designated level of performance.

Bridging the Gap: Serving Multiple Assessment Purposes

The Early Literacy Profile (New York State Education Department 1999), parts of which are shown in the figures below, is an example of how these multiple purposes for assessment can be met. *The Early Literacy Profile* (ELP) is an assessment system designed to provide information about elementary students' progress in the language arts at both the individual and group level. It is standardized enough to be used for accountability purposes, yet flexible enough to be responsive to individual learning differences (Falk and Ort 1999). It is made up of a small set of standardized tasks—a set each for reading, writing, and oral language—which are to be completed by students during the everyday life of their classroom and collected at two times in the school year (see Figure 4–5).

While each task in each section of the ELP has a specified format and criteria, the content and context in which the information is collected can vary according to the situation and the needs of the students. What is standardized is the format and the way that the evidence is evaluated. In the reading section, for example, the format is standardized by requiring three pieces of evidence: a reading interview conducted by the teacher, using a form to list specific student skills and behaviors (see Figure 4–6); a reading list filled out by the student (see Figure 4–7); and a student-written response to a text (see Figure 4–8). Together, these three pieces of evidence are assessed in relation to a reading scale containing descriptions of the standards' key qualities, as they are demonstrated by students at different stages along a continuum of development (see Figure 4–9). The reading scale describes eight different stages.

The points of development represented by each stage of the reading scale have been determined through a combination of factors, including what research and theory tell us is appropriate for human learning as well as what has actually been observed in a representative sample of children for this age group. Based on references to these factors, the ELP offers a guide to what stages teachers should reasonably expect children to attain by the end of each grade (see Figure 4–10).

Determining what scale score to assign a student involves making a judgment about what stage in the scale best describes a student's work. Teachers do this by matching the evidence of students' abilities as seen in students' work samples with the descriptions of the qualities found in the scales. Although students may frequently demonstrate different levels of proficiency for different qualities of their work, teachers determine what stage the student has arrived at by making an overall judgment, based on examining all the work, that best reflects where the

ELP Reading and Writing

Reading Evidence

Students' reading proficiencies are assessed by examining these three pieces of evidence:

1. Reading Sample to analyze
   - Fluency
   - Comprehension
2. Reading List to provide evidence about students' range and experience as readers
3. Reading Response to provide additional information about students' abilities to understand and analyze texts

Writing Evidence

Students' abilities to use written language to express ideas and to communicate effectively are assessed by examining three forms of evidence:

✔ Story/narrative—first draft
✔ Story/narrative—second draft OR another first draft of a different writing samples (for students in early stages of writing development)
✔ Reading Response—the same one that was completed for the Reading Evidence section

---

Figure 4–5   ©2000 by Beverly Falk from *The Heart of the Matter*, Portsmouth, NH: Heinemann

body of evidence most fully resides. This process enables the assessment to produce a single score that can be used for reporting purposes.

To illustrate how the scoring works, note these samples of six-year-old Robin's writing, his responses to literature and a story (see Figures 4–11 and 4–12). Together, they were used as the evidence for assigning him a score of 2, or *Advanced Emergent Writer*, on the writing scale (see Figure 4–13).

Even though not all the descriptions in the Advanced Emergent Writer column matched what was found in Robin's work (for example, his writing did in a sense have a topic or theme, which is described as a characteristic of Early Beginning Writer or scale point 3), his teacher decided that a 2 was the best description of where the *bulk* of the evidence collected about him most fully resided.

Reading Sample

Name: _____ Grade: _____ **Side 1**

Left vertical label: **Fluency**

Date	FALL (/ /)		SPRING (/ /)	
Title/Author				

Type of Text
(Each type of text correlates with a scale point on the reading scale.)

FALL / SPRING:
1. Simple picture book 2. Patterned language / picture book
3. Easy beginning reader / short chapter / content-area book 4. Beginning reader / short content-area book
5. Easy chapter / content-area book 6. Medium-level chapter /content-area book
7. Challenging children's literature 8. Complex children's literature

	Rate (Fall)	Comments:	Rate (Spring)	Comments:
Engaged in pretend reading	1 2 3 4		1 2 3 4	
Used book language	1 2 3 4		1 2 3 4	
Understood directionality of print	1 2 3 4		1 2 3 4	
Focused on print	1 2 3 4		1 2 3 4	
Understood concept of word	1 2 3 4		1 2 3 4	
Drew on previous experience to make sense of text	1 2 3 4		1 2 3 4	
Used pictures to aid understanding	1 2 3 4		1 2 3 4	
Recognized high-frequency words in text	1 2 3 4		1 2 3 4	
Had a substantial sight vocabulary with few miscues	1 2 3 4		1 2 3 4	
Used graphophonic strategies: Beginning consonants / root words / endings / syllabication	1 2 3 4		1 2 3 4	
Used syntactic strategies: Predictable language patterns / sentence and grammatical structure	1 2 3 4		1 2 3 4	
Used semantic strategies: picture clues / recall of story line	1 2 3 4		1 2 3 4	
Used a variety of cueing systems	1 2 3 4		1 2 3 4	
Was independent in resolving text difficulties	1 2 3 4		1 2 3 4	
Monitored own reading	1 2 3 4		1 2 3 4	
Self-corrected	1 2 3 4		1 2 3 4	
Projected meaning with oral expression	1 2 3 4		1 2 3 4	
Maintained momentum and fluency	1 2 3 4		1 2 3 4	
Demonstrated confidence	1 2 3 4		1 2 3 4	

Rating Key: 1 = Not at All 2 = A Little 3 = Moderately 4 = A Lot   If a choice does not apply, write N/A (not applicable) in the "comments" space.

Figure 4–6. Evidence Section Descriptions ELP Reading Interview Form

Reading Sample

Comprehension

	FALL (/)		SPRING (/)	
	Rate	Comments:	Rate	Comments:
Described characters	1 2 3 4		1 2 3 4	
Identified setting	1 2 3 4		1 2 3 4	
Identified main idea or problem	1 2 3 4		1 2 3 4	
Explained resolution of problem	1 2 3 4		1 2 3 4	
Retold story / summarized text	1 2 3 4		1 2 3 4	
Sequenced events	1 2 3 4		1 2 3 4	
Recalled relevant details and/or events	1 2 3 4		1 2 3 4	
Analyzed, interpreted, made inferences	1 2 3 4		1 2 3 4	
Commented on literary aspects of text —genre, images	1 2 3 4		1 2 3 4	
Noticed nuances, subtleties of text	1 2 3 4		1 2 3 4	
Related text to other ideas or experiences	1 2 3 4		1 2 3 4	
Made predictions and/or conclusions	1 2 3 4		1 2 3 4	

Suggestions for further instruction and support:

RATING KEY

Note the degree to which the student used the behavior, strategy, or characteristic:

1 = Not at all 4 = A lot
2 = A little If a choice does not apply, write N/A (not applicable) in the "comments" space.
3 = Moderately

Figure 4-6. (Continued)

_____'s Reading List

FALL

Date	Title and Author	Type of Text (fiction, nonfiction, poetry, etc.)	I read this book: alone	with an adult	with a partner or group	Reading this book was: easy	just right	hard	My Opinion 1-didn't like 2-okay 3-good 4-great	Comments
1.										
2.										
3.										
4.										
5.										

Figure 4–7.   ELP Student Reading List Form

Reading Response

Choose a text that you have read. Write a letter to a friend about this text.

In the letter:
• Tell your friend what the text was about.
• Discuss one part that you liked or didn't like.
• Tell your friend why you think she/he would like (or not like) this text.

Title:_____

Author:_____

Reading this book was:

☐ easy
☐ just right
☐ hard

I read this book:

☐ alone
☐ with an adult
☐ with a partner or group

Today's date: _____

Dear _____,

....

....

....

....

....

....

Early Literacy Profile

Figure 4–8.   ELP Student-Written Response to a Text Form

Reading Scale

Name: _____ Grade: _____

	Emergent Reader		Beginning Reader		Independent Reader		Experienced Reader	
	1 Early Emergent Reader	2 Advanced Emergent Reader	3 Early Beginning Reader	4 Advanced Beginning Reader	5 Early Independent Reader	6 Advanced Independent Reader	7 Experienced	8 Very Experienced
Type of text that student reads at instructional level	Simple picture books: • Text generally focuses on a single idea. • Words in text are large, well-spaced with only one or two lines on each page. • Words or sentence patterns in text are repeated. • A simple illustration or picture accompanies and directly corresponds to the text. • Texts are brief ranging from 10–36 words • Examples of these types of books are The Birthday Cake (The Wright Group) and Colors.	Simple texts/Patterned language / picture books: • Text may contain rhyming, repetitive words, phrases, and actions in predictable language structures. • Pictures provide much of the main idea. • Text range from 25–70 words. • Examples of these kinds of books are My Garden (Scholastic) and Fun with Hats (Mondo).	Core easy patterned language books/Easy beginning reader/ short chapter/content area books: • Illustrations provide important information about the text. • There are many high frequency words. • Text begins to introduce simple plot, theme, problems and/or solutions. • Repetition of events and/or words is in each of the stories. • Natural language patterns begin to appear. • Text generally consists of several lines per page. • Examples of these kinds of books are Brown Bear (Martin) and Go Dog Go (Eastman).	Beginning reader/ short chapter/content area books: • Illustrations support the text. • There are many high frequency words. • Text has simple theme, plot, and problems and/or solutions. • Some repetition of events in each of the stories. • Natural language patterns are incorporated. • Text generally consists of several lines per page. • Examples of these kinds of books are Nosy Nora (Wells) and More Spaghetti I Say.	Easy chapter/content area books: • Texts may have illustrations that provide moderate to minimum support. • Text has clearly evident theme or plot with conclusions. • Examples of these books are Nate the Great to Madeline (Bemelmans).	Medium level chapter/content area books: • Texts have illustrations that provide minimal to incidental support. • Increasingly complex information, plot line, character or relationships. • Literary language structures are integrated with natural language. • Examples of these kinds of books range from The Stories Julian Tells to Freckle Juice.	Challenging children's literature: • Occasional pictures enhance the story. • Language structures and vocabulary are increasingly complex. • Background knowledge and higher-level thinking skills may be needed to understand and appreciate the humor, the problem, or the suspense. • Chapters build upon each other. • Text size is usually a bit smaller. • Examples of these kinds of books range from Amber Brown is not a Crayon to Little House on the Prairie.	Complex children's literature: • Texts may not have any illustrations. • Text addresses issues and/or information with shades of meaning requiring interpretation and analysis. • Imagery and metaphors may be used. • Chapters may move in time, place, and perspective. • Examples of these kinds of texts range from Charlie and the Chocolate Factory to Roll of Thunder, Hear My Cry.
Strategies	• Begins to display awareness of some conventions of print: front-back of book, left-right. • Focuses mainly on pictures. • Begins to know difference between pictures and print. • May recognize familiar words occasionally. • May engage in "pretend" reading. • Assistance and much support from adult is needed.	• Awareness of conventions of print is established: front-back of book, left-right progression, top-bottom. • Focuses on pictures as well as print. • Known difference between pictures and print and begins to demonstrate awareness of one-one correspondence. • Knows a few familiar words on sight. • May engage in "pretend" reading, using book language ("once upon a time," "the end," etc.). • May "read" from memory. • May draw upon predictable language patterns to anticipate or recall the text. • May demonstrate awareness of some letter-sound relationships mostly beginning consonants. • Assistance and much support from adult is needed.	• Focuses mostly on the print to decipher meaning. • Picture clues still provide crucial support. • One-to-one correspondence is fairly established. • Small sight-word vocabulary is established. • Some high frequency words in text are recognized. • Begins to use some aspects of cueing systems: letter-sound relationships (especially beginning and ending consonants, root words), recall of story line, and predictable language structures. • Starts to monitor and self-correct own reading. • Reading requires considerable effort and continued assistance from adult.	• Focuses on print to decipher meaning, refers to pictures only for support. • Stable sight vocabulary is established. • High frequency words are recognized. • Uses wider range of cueing systems while reading, sometimes with prompting from adult. • Monitoring and self-correcting are becoming established. • Reading requires some effort and assistance from adult.	• Begins to use cueing systems to problem-solve text difficulties with increasing independence. • Substantial sight vocabulary is established. • Monitoring and self-correcting are used regularly. • Oral reading begins to have some momentum. • Expression begins to be evident in oral reading. • Developing confidence and independence as a reader.	• Uses all cueing systems independently to problem-solve occasionally encountered text difficulties. • Recognizes most words in text. • Monitoring and self-correcting are used regularly and quickly to solve problems. • Oral reading has momentum and fluency. • Demonstrates increasing confidence and independence as a reader.	• Cueing systems are mostly internalized. • Few word problems encountered during reading. • Problem-solving strategies are mostly internalized. • Oral reading has momentum and fluency. • Effective oral expression and attention to punctuation. • Demonstrates confidence and independence.	• Cueing systems are almost entirely internalized. • Problems are encountered rarely during reading. • Problem-solving strategies are internalized. • Oral expression during reading reflects the subtleties of mood, pace and tension of text. • Demonstrates strong sense of confidence and independence. • Reading pace and stamina is strong.
Comprehension	• Uses pictures almost exclusively to gain understanding. • Can talk about the pictures	• Relies mostly on pictures clues and recall of story line to make sense of print. • Demonstrates understanding of a story through comments, reactions, discussion, and/or drawings.	• Relies more on print to find the meaning of text, but pictures play an important role. • Can identify some of the attributes in the text: character, setting, problem, resolution. • Retells general story or subject of text, but awareness of sequence of events may not be demonstrated.	• Relies mainly on print to find meaning of text with pictures playing a supporting role. • Can identify and discuss many of the attributes in the text: characters, setting, problem and resolution • Retells and discusses story or subject of text with some awareness of sequence of events.	• Can identify and discuss characters, setting, problem and resolution. • Retells and discusses story or subject of text with awareness of sequence of events.	• Can identify and discuss characters, setting, problem resolution. • Retells and discusses subject of text with awareness of sequence of events and attention to relevant details.	• Can provide a coherent synthesis of the meaning of the text, using relevant details. • Analysis and interpretation skills are developing. • Awareness of the literary aspects of text and/or nuances and subtleties of text is developing. • May relate ideas in text to other ideas, experiences, and/or literature when prompted.	• Can provide a coherent synthesis of the meaning of the text, with extensive use of relevant details. • Appreciates nuances and subtleties of text. • Has strong awareness of literacy aspects of text. • Can volunteer independently how ideas in text relate to other ideas, experiences, and/or literature.

Figure 4–9 ELP Reading Scale

ELP Correlational Guide

Grade	Reasonable Expectations for Reading/Writing*
Prekindergarten	Emergent: Early or Advanced
Kindergarten	Advanced Emergent
First Grade	Beginning: Early or Advanced
Second Grade	Advanced Beginning or Early Independent
Third Grade	Independent: Early or Advanced
Fourth Grade and Above	Experiences and Very Experienced

*Based on findings from spring 1998 pilot administration

Figure 4–10   ©2000 by Beverly Falk from *The Heart of the Matter*, Portsmouth, NH: Heinemann

Teachers learn how to determine scores by practicing with their colleagues on common sets of student work. They discuss together how students' work demonstrates different proficiencies, matching the evidence with the standards in the scales, until they come to consensus about what score is the best description for each child. Through this process, teachers learn a lot about what strategies, skills, and behaviors to look for and support in their students. As they do this, they also develop common understandings of what constitutes quality work. The more they talk about student work, the stronger their shared definitions become. When New York State teachers scored student work together in teams for *The Early Literacy Profile*, it was found that the score given by the teacher who was unfamiliar with the child and had seen only the child's work matched the score given by the child's teacher well over 80 percent of the time (Falk and Ort 1998).

The tasks that make up *The Early Literacy Profile* do not intrude on classroom work in the way that many tests generally do. Even though they have a standardized format, they are administered in the natural context of the classroom. Likewise, preparation for administering the ELP is less of an intrusion than the preparation for many standardized tests. Students do not have to learn tricks or test strategies. Because the assessment examines real-life reading and writing, the best preparation is simply to engage in real-life reading and writing activities.

Reading Response

Title The EAR BOOK

Author A LiPERKiNS

This book was: ☑ Easy ☐ Just right ☐ Hard
I read this book: ☑ Alone ☐ With an adult ☐ With a partner ☐ With a group

UANI5
(today's date)

Dear MAFUNN
iLRDHoD PLAED
FOT

Sincerely,

ROBiN

(I learned how to play the flute)

Figure 4–11. Robin's response to literature

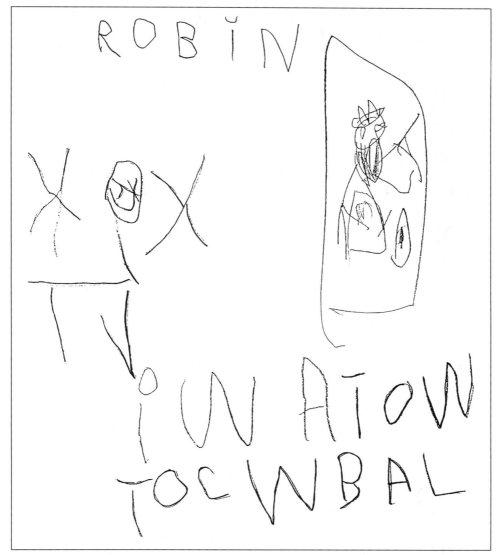

Figure 4–12.　Robin's story

Writing Scale

Name: _____ Grade: _____

	Emergent Writer		Beginner Reader		Independent Writer		Experienced Reader	
	1 Early Emergent Writer	2 Advanced Emergent Writer	3 Early Beginning Writer	4 Advanced Beginning Writer	5 Early Independent Writer	6 Advanced Independent Writer	7 Experienced	8 Very Experienced
Idea Development and Language Use	• Idea(s) conveyed through picture(s) and possibly minimal letter or words • Pictures/symbols used primarily	• Idea is conveyed through pictures and words • Pictures and words are used (i.e., may label a picture)	• Topic/theme is developing • Words are strung together in sentence format • Names and "favorite" words are repeated	• Topic/theme is evident • Uses simple, repetitive sentences • Uses simple, repetitive vocabulary • May "mimic" sentence patterns and/or ideas as seen in other texts	• Main idea/topic/theme is established, supported by some detail • Begins to vary sentence pattern • Vocabulary includes some descriptive words • Sense of voice/audience may begin to appear	• Main idea/topic/theme is established, supported by ample detail • Varied sentence patterns are common • Vocabulary includes ample descriptive words • Sense of voice/audience is developing	• Main idea/topic/theme is established with relationships developing to other ideas/themes • Ideas connect to give indication of point of view/sense of content and/or characters • Ideas are presented and developed with supporting details • Ample use of varied language and sentence patterns • Uses varied and descriptive vocabulary • Sense of voice is established • Writes to an appropriate audience	• Main idea/topic theme is established with relationships established to other ideas/themes • Ideas connect to clearly present point of view, content, and/or characters • Ideas are presented, developed, and elaborated fully using many supportive details • Leaves out details that are not relevant • Uses varied and elegant language and sentence patterns • Uses varied, descriptive and lively vocabulary • Effective use of strategies such as dialogue and suspense • Expressive, individual voice • Writes engagingly to an appropriate audience
Organization	• No organization is evident	• Begins to use left/right and top/bottom orientation	• Left/right and top/bottom orientation is established	• Sentences are structured around theme although may not be in logical/sequential order	• Writing is structured out theme and has evidence of beginning, middle, and end	• Writing is structured around theme and has clear beginning/middle/end • Writing is easy to understand and follow	• Ideas are presented in clear order and logical sequence that makes use of some of the following: paragraphs, transitions, introductions, conclusions	• Ideas are presented in clear order and logical sequence that makes use of ample use of the following: paragraphs, transitions, introductions, conclusions • Writing has distinctive organizing shape, structure and focus
Conventions	• Makes marks and random letters to represent ideas/words	• Reproduces words from signs and other sources in environment • May represent a whole word with one or a few letters • Uses sound-symbol linkages, relying heavily on most obvious sounds of a word (i.e., beginning consonants)	• Legible writing with recognizable words • Uses mix of capital and lower case letters • Spacing between words is evident • Spells words phonetically	• Legible writing with recognizable sentences • Mix between conventional and phonetic spelling • Punctuation, capitalization, and upper/lower case letters are in use sometimes	• Conventional spelling, punctuation, capitalization, and upper/lower case letters are used often	• Conventional spelling, punctuation, capitalization, and upper/lower case letters are solidly established	• Simple conventions are under control • Complex conventions - such as complicated structure and grammar - appear	• Simple conventions are under control • Complex conventions gain elegance and are increasingly evident

Figure 4–13   ELP Writing Scale

Benefits of Standards-Based Performance Assessments

- Clarify goals and expectations for teaching
- Provide a clear and coherent vision of desired goals
- Guide teaching toward key concepts and critical issues in different areas of knowledge
- Offer educators opportunities to think about curricula and teaching strategies that can be used to improve instruction
- Allow for a variety of ways for students to demonstrate what they know and can do
- Level the playing field for all students by providing everyone with access to the same expectations and images of accomplished work
- Provide teachers with insights about students—what they know and can do as well as how they do it—to reveal areas of strength as well those in need of support
- Inform teachers, students, families, communities, and educational authorities about student achievement of specific criteria rather than just how students perform in relation to others
- Reveal progress of individuals as well as groups to give an accurate picture of the value added by the teachers and schools in which students have had their educational experience
- Identify inequalities in access to learning opportunities and supports
- Establish the shared meanings and common language that are needed to create a professional community in support of improved learning

Figure 4–14   ©2000 by Beverly Falk from *The Heart of the Matter*, Portsmouth, NH: Heinemann

In these ways, *The Early Literacy Profile* and other standards-based performance assessments bridge the long-standing gap between assessment used for evaluation and accountability and assessment used for inquiry to support meaningful learning. Standards-based performance assessments support teaching by providing teachers with a guide for their teaching and with information about *what* students can do as well as *how* they do it. They support student learning by offering students opportunities to demonstrate their understandings in a variety of ways and, because of their open and clear expectations, by giving students a fair shot at demonstrating what they know. At the same time, standards-based performance assessments are useful accountability measures because they allow the public to see student and school progress in relation to valued goals.

Chapter 5

Possibilities and Problems of
a Standards-Based Approach

The Good, the Bad, and the Ugly

As the standards movement has proliferated, it has been criticized from a variety of perspectives for a range of reasons. Because so many of these criticisms raise important issues that when not attended to result in harmful practices for children, teachers, and our profession as a whole, let us explore some of the critiques below. They have to do with the content and nature of standards, the locus of standards, the kinds of tests used to assess achievement of standards, the ways that standards are being used in accountability systems, and what is needed to ensure that standards are achieved.

Problems with the Content and Nature of Standards

Among the criticisms leveled at the standards movement is the charge that it is a "one-size-fits-all approach" (Ohanian 1999). Those holding this view chafe at the idea that all children need to learn the same things (externally imposed standards), in the same way, at the same pace, and then get tested on these standards through high-stakes, norm-referenced, standardized tests. They see this way of conducting schooling as an "autocratic, regimented throw-back to factory-model approaches to schooling, where students are forced to regurgitate expert-prescribed sets of facts or face failure" (Thompson 1999, 46).

One-size-fits-all approaches to learning are, indeed, problematic. They do not take into consideration the fact that children learn and develop in highly individual and idiosyncratic ways and that, because of this, attempts to have everyone learn the same things in the same ways at the same pace will therefore surely end in failure for a significant proportion of students (NAEYC 1988). Approaches like these ignore all we have learned about the multiple intelligences humans possess, the different pathways that exist to understanding and mastery that are effective for some and not for others, and the varied paces, styles, and modes of learning found in different individuals (Gardner 1983; Sternberg 1985).

The one-size-fits-all interpretation of standards, however, is only one of many that go by the name of standards-based reform. The standards movement is, in fact, in no way monolithic. It includes a vast and varied array of advocates, practitioners, and policy makers whose views and practices are as diverse as the students for whom they have been created. The standards movement includes, for example, advocates of national standards and corresponding national tests (Ravitch 1995; Tucker and Codding 1998) as well as opponents of national standards and tests (Darling-Hammond 1994a). It encompasses those who view standards as a means to enforce more and tougher expectations for students (Hirsch 1996) as well as those who see standards as a means to change the nature of expectations for students in order to improve the quality of learning that goes on in classrooms and schools (Alvarado 1998; Darling-Hammond and Falk 1997b; Kohn 1999; O'Neil and Tell 1999; Resnick 1995; Resnick and Hall 1998; Resnick and Resnick 1991). The first interpretation of standards confuses *harder* with *better*. It defines higher standards in terms of mastering *more* and *more difficult* content— memorizing more state capitals, dates, and facts; getting students to work harder to bring up their grades. The latter interpretation defines higher standards in terms of developing a deeper, richer, more engaging curriculum in which students play an active role in integrating ideas and in pursuing controversial questions.

Still other perspectives on standards criticizes the standards movement for not going far enough in delineating what content and skills students should learn in each subject at every grade (American Federation of Teachers 1997). In contrast, some have criticized many standards for articulating too narrowly what students should learn and what they should be expected to demonstrate at certain ages, thus dictating how teachers teach. Those who hold this latter view propose that standards should serve as a means for educational stakeholders to find common ground only about the essentials of learning. They worry that standards are being articulated in such a detailed and encompassing way that people are losing sight of what a reasonable and full education entails. They fear that the combined expectations of all the different standards in all the different fields are becoming humanly impossible to achieve (Darling-Hammond 1997; Gagnon 1994; Kohn 1999; Perrone 1999). "The Mid-continent Regional Educational Laboratory has even estimated that it would take 6,000 extra hours of classroom time to cover all the information required on most state standards, roughly the same amount of time that it takes to earn a master's degree" (Stoskopf 2000, 38).

More controversies associated with standards have to do with the perspective they reflect about multiculturalism. One critique is that some standards lack sensitivity to issues of race, culture, and gender (Berlak 1995; Marzano and Kendall 1996; Purpel 1995; White House Initiative on Educational Excellence for Hispanic Americans 1999). This lack of sensitivity can be manifested in either excluding content that is important to different races and cultures or in defining expectations in such a way that they are biased toward specific ethnic, linguistic, or socioeconomic groups. This particular charge is illustrated by examining some of the expectations articulated in social studies and English language arts standards documents from states around the country. Many of these documents deemphasize the contributions of different racial or ethnic groups or devalue the unique expressive styles of different ethnic or linguistic groups that affect the way they answer questions.

An opposing critique of standards, however, claims just the opposite. It raises the criticism that some standards place too much emphasis on multicultural issues and events and, as a result, ignore too many important traditional figures and events in our country (Porter, A. 1995).

These sets of criticisms caution us to beware of the different interpretations of standards and to take care to embrace only those initiatives that reflect shared beliefs and worthy goals (Darling-Hammond 1997; Darling-Hammond and Falk 1997b; Falk and Ort 1998; Kohn 1999). We need to avoid standards defined in ways that repeat the worst mistakes of the competency-based education movements of the 1970s: those that specified hundreds of discrete objectives that reduce subject matter to so many tiny sub-skills and facts that they are too reductionistic to be useful for thoughtful teaching. We need to guard against an approach to standards that leaves teachers with little room to create exciting and interesting curricula that is responsive to students' needs or that does not allow opportunities to integrate important ideas between and among disciplines.

Instead, we should seek standards-based initiatives that assist us in articulating core ideas and critical skills, in and across disciplines, in a way that is sufficiently pointed to be meaningful for guiding practice without being overly prescriptive. We need standards that shift the focus of what happens in classrooms to more meaningful problem solving, more performance-oriented learning, the pursuit of deeper understanding, and the valuing of diverse ways of pursuing and demonstrating knowledge. We need standards that define expectations in age-appropriate ways—broad intellectual competencies that are reasonable expectations for children within certain age spans—rather than narrowly defined expectations for children to acquire specific facts and skills by the completion of each grade. We need to use these standards as opportunities for educational communities to clarify expectations as well as to develop shared meanings and language about these expectations.

Problems with Top-Down versus Bottom-Up Standards

Another key area of concern raised about standards is the issue of who should create them. Differences exist about what organizational level is most appropriate for the development and enforcement of meaningful standards; about whether standards should be generated by individuals, by schools, or by local, state, or federal agencies. Some believe that standards should be nationally produced and nationally assessed in much the same way that other countries celebrated for their academic excellence organize their educational systems (Fitzgerald 1979; Ravitch 1995). They believe that schooling in the United States, which has no national curriculum—although some would argue that the textbook industry has created a defacto one (Apple 1995)—would be strengthened greatly by national standards enforced with national tests as they are in France, Great Britain, China, and Japan.

Unlike other countries, however, educational policy and implementation in the United States has historically been the purview of the states. Because of this, many argue that state education departments are the most appropriate entity to take on standards development and assessment redesign initiatives. The experiences of states that have pioneered standards-based reforms (such as Kentucky, Vermont, California, Maryland, Delaware, and New York) suggests that state-level approaches to school improvement, while providing a focusing effect, are not a panacea. There is no automatic guarantee that state standards, along with the teaching practices they strive to inspire, will make their way into the lives of teachers and students in meaningful and useful ways (Ort 1999).

It is for this reason that many who have engaged in school-based reforms are against imposing external standards as a means to improve schools. They worry that state standards will become mandates used to routinize and regiment teaching processes, forcing teachers to follow uniform and "teacher-proof" curricula. And when state standards get connected to high-stakes tests—tests that are used to make important decisions about students' futures—fears such as these are further increased. High-stakes tests, with sanctions and rewards such as promotion, retention, placement into groups or tracks, graduation, or withholding a diploma, can easily drive curricula to be narrowed and distorted as a result of having to prepare students to perform well on them.

Because of these issues, many school reformers argue against standards imposed from afar. They prefer only standard-setting efforts that are local. They believe that local, context-embedded conversations about teaching, students, and their work are the most effective mechanism for deep instructional change (Sizer 1995). To support their views, they point to the nationally acclaimed successes of such urban schools serving diverse populations as the Central Park East Schools, Urban Academy, and International High School in New York City—schools that have created their own local processes to carry out innovative changes in teaching, learning, and organizational structures.

The examples of excellence represented by those schools are indeed powerful and do provide us with images and models of what is possible. These are, however, far from the rule in this nation of 85,000 public schools. Can we rely solely on this locally developed and locally monitored approach to standards? Can we hope that by asking educators to voluntarily create their own standards in their schools we can accomplish the task of ensuring that the quality of teaching and learning be raised for *all* children across *all* schools—regardless of what part of town a given school is located in, what the socioeconomic makeup of its student body is, or what talents and expertise its faculty possess?

It is because of the enormity of the difficulties posed by such systemic change that externally developed, standards-based approaches to school improvement have been initiated. By attempting to get educational stakeholders to create and enforce consensus across a state or district about some key expectations for all students (a significant departure from past practices when whole categories of students were "tracked" into programs with dumbed-down curricula) standards-based approaches have sought to guarantee that *all* children are well served by schools.

Standards-based approaches to schooling can provide teachers with a common point of reference—a framework to shape curriculum, teaching, and assessment. In so doing they have the potential to maintain quality control while still allowing schools the freedom and the authority to make important decisions about how instructional and assessment practices should be used. Standards-based approaches can actually free schools to vary their practices to meet the diverse needs of their student populations. The same standards can be taught through project-based learning out in the community or through direct instruction in the classroom, depending on the school's orientation and the teachers' experience, confidence, creativity, or inspiration. By holding all students to common expectations, standards can be an impetus for providing educators with the tools, processes, opportunities, and supports that are needed to help students across the socioeconomic spectrum reach for and achieve high levels of performance according to their multiple intelligences and dreams.

Standards-based approaches to school improvement that are undertaken in this spirit represent a shift from other approaches to improvement that have dominated the twentieth century. "The shift is from high expectations for *some* to high expectations for *all*; from a focus on coverage to a focus on results; from monitoring seat time and methods to monitoring performance; from a focus on quantity to a focus on quality; from a focus on grades to a focus on student work" (Thompson 1999, 49). And this is where the potential resides for powerful learning to be experienced by all who are engaged in standards-based efforts. Standards-based initiatives, no matter whether they are locally or externally derived, challenge everyone to engage in the same kind of rich conversations about learning to which the educators at the Central Park East Schools, Urban Academy, and International High School have attributed their success. Everyone engaged in standards-based work is pressed to seek answers to such questions as: What is a quality performance? What does it mean for a student to perform to standards? How good is good enough? What instructional strategies and supports are needed to ensure that all students meet the standards? What will be required—of teachers, of schools, of parents, and of the system—to help those students who have not yet met a given standard after repeated attempts to do so? Using standards to situate the enterprise of schooling in a common framework across districts and states, educators involved in standards-based work can be stimulated to reflect on what they do and to develop their own distinctive and unique educational philosophies, practices, and cultures.

No autocratic, regimented, heavy-handed bureaucratic approach to schooling ever provoked questions and actions like these. Nor did any allow, indeed encourage, educators to vary their instructional strategies, call on their many creativities, and utilize many pathways to arrive at a common destination. For every person, policy, and practice in the system, standards-based reforms, if used in these ways, can have transformational implications.

Problems with Testing and Accountability

Unfortunately, merely establishing standards for content and performance at a state or district level does not guarantee that the standards—no matter how worthy—will be translated into practice or that people will use them in ways that lead to better teaching and learning. Neither does establishing standards guarantee that the standards will be achieved. Recognizing this, a host of policies have been initiated by policy makers intended to hold schools accountable for realizing the goals articulated in their respective standards. These policy initiatives usually include mandated assessments, public reporting of school, district, and/or student performance on these assessments, and systems of test-related rewards, sanctions, and interventions for students and educators alike.

In the best of cases, assessments used for accountability purposes are designed around standards that are challenging. These kinds of tests have significant portions that utilize performance formats, providing students with opportunities to demonstrate their knowledge and skills and to explain their understandings. Assessed in relation to the standards, these standards-based performance tests are a significant improvement over those that test students against each other and are made up solely of multiple-choice, fill in the blank, or true/false items. In spite of growing consensus around this fact however, at least twenty-five states that claim to be implementing new standards still use old-style norm-referenced tests (*Education USA* 1999).

Assessing New Standards with Old Tests

One of the reasons that new standards are still being assessed by old tests is that test development is expensive, especially development of standards-based tests. It is expensive because it presents enormous technical challenges in regard to design and scoring and because it also poses significant resource and time demands both on students as well as scorers. Because of these issues, many states and districts that are enacting new standards have been reluctant to develop the more sophisticated assessment instruments that can help make standards "stick." Instead, they simply take generic commercially developed tests "off the shelf," match up test items to their standards, and announce that the tests have been "customized" to evaluate student progress in relation to the standards' articulated expectations.

The problem with doing this is that the nature of many of these tests remains unchanged. Because these so-called standards-based tests continue to evaluate in norm-referenced ways, they allow the predetermined patterns of success, inherent in all norm-referenced tests, to stay intact. Because they generally contain few performance items and their formats provide little opportunities for higher-order thinking to be expressed, they do little to influence teaching and learning to focus on higher-order skills and knowledge. This approach to testing the standards leaves the standards at risk of becoming little more than words.

Technical Problems in Test Development Undermine Public Trust

But even when the exams to measure standards are actually designed around the standards, and even when they utilize performance formats that point practice in the direction of more meaningful and deeper knowledge, problems with the standards-based tests themselves have arisen that undermine public trust in standards-based reforms. In Kentucky, which created a system of standards-based reforms coupled with performance assessments to which high-stakes consequences for teachers and schools are attached, complications related to the reliability of the assessments have led to a partial dismantling of the new system and a reversion to multiple-choice, norm-referenced tests. Other problems with the accuracy and validity of test results have led to serious questioning of standards-based reforms. In California, New York, and other states, test publishers have made a series of technical errors in constructing and/or scoring the exams. An error in the scoring of New York City's new 1999 reading tests improperly lowered the test scores to below "passing" for thousands of children. Because the schools' chancellor had previously mandated that students who scored below "passing" were not to be promoted to the next grade, all of these children were incorrectly barred from moving on to the next grade!

Such travesties raise still other issues that can make the difference between standards-based reforms being helpful or hurtful. Both the role tests play in the accountability system and the stakes that are attached to their results can dramatically affect whether even the best-designed tests can do harm or can do good.

High-Stakes Testing Causes Harm

Many states and districts around the country are reporting student performance in school report cards or in ranking lists that are published in the newspapers. These results then carry consequences for students, school personnel, and schools.

High test scores have always reaped rewards for students in the form of placement in high tracks or groups—honors or Advanced Placement courses, reading groups, and so on—which then qualifies them for admittance to special opportunities and/or, eventually, elite colleges. The recent national push for high standards and accountability, however, has seen the institution of additional incentives. In some districts and states children are being offered actual dollar rewards for reading books or attaining high test scores. Other places are offering students free or reduced college tuition in exchange for achieving high scores on tests (National Center for Fair and Open Testing 1999).

Low test scorers, on the other hand, are currently facing unprecedented "tough" consequences for their performance. Despite the substantial body of evidence that points to the harmful effects of retaining students in a grade, and despite the urgings of national experts and commissions to rely less on standardized testing and more on broader measures of student progress when making high-stakes decisions about students' lives, many districts are enacting "no promotion" policies for those students who do not meet the proficiency standard set as passing for their tests (International Reading Association 1999; Koretz 1996; Linn 1996; Madaus 1989; National Council on Education, Standards, and Testing 1992). These retention policies, in turn, lead to increases in special education placements as well as in high school dropout rates (Darling-Hammond and Falk 1997b).

Eighteen states and the District of Columbia now link promotion to performance on state exams. And thirteen of those states also require some form of intervention, such as summer school, for students at risk of failing. Tens of thousands of students are being enrolled in what has become virtually a nationwide effort to end what is referred to as "social promotion"—the automatic promotion of students to the next grade (White and Johnston 1999).

About half of the nation's big-city systems that are threatening not to promote students who do not meet the proficiency standard of their state exams offered remedial summer school during the summer of 1999. In many of them (Chicago, Houston, Oakland, Denver, Washington, D.C., and New York City, to name just a few) attendance was mandatory. Although the long-range results of these programs are not yet known, those that appear, in the short-term, to be successful emphasize deep and meaningful instruction and offer small classes, creative lessons, and individual attention. Those that appear to be most successful do not threaten students with being held back in a grade if an end-of-summer test is not passed. Those programs that focus predominantly on drilling students for a high-stakes test that will determine if a student moves on to the next grade often succeed in elevating test scores but, in the long run, are of questionable benefit. As one researcher on this topic was quoted in a recent review:

> A well-designed summer school program can be of great benefit to students. But student test gains do not maintain over time if there is not better overall instruction during the school year. (White and Johnston 1999, 8)

Sanctions and Rewards Increasing for Teachers and Schools Based on Students' Tests Scores

Students are not the only targets of high-stakes test pressures. Teachers and administrators too are under intense scrutiny and are being offered performance sanctions and rewards. Many states and districts are tying salary increases to the student test scores of individual teachers. Kentucky, for example, gives teachers rewards for the performance of their students on state tests. In some districts, superintendents are receiving bonuses of as much as $30,000 or more for each year during their tenure that test scores go up. In addition, contract continuation decisions for school personnel are frequently being tied to student test performance.

These policies of sanctions and rewards are also being extended to whole schools. In Chicago, teachers and principals can be reassigned if their schools do not perform well on district tests. And in New York State, a "takeover" policy has been established to close down low-performing schools, removing administrators and teachers, and then reopening them with a new name or number as well as with a new cadre of teachers and administrators. The new staff is generally given only two to three years to bring up the test scores or lose their positions (White and Johnston 1999).

Intended and Unintended Negative Consequences of High-Stakes Tests

These various measures impact on schools in both positive and negative ways. To some degree, external pressures, like state mandates and public reporting of test scores, appear to have a focusing effect. They increase public, press, and school attention to student performance and help overcome forces that seek to maintain the status quo. The most positive effects have been found, however, in states like Maryland and Maine where the consequences for test results are not so severe; in other words, they do not keep students from graduating or moving on to the next grade (Clotfeller and Ladd 1996; Elmore 1996; Elmore, Abelmann, and Fuhrman 1996; Firestone, Mayrowetz, and Fairman 1997; Murnane and Levy 1996).

Teaching to the Test

Significant drawbacks have been noted across the range of states where test performance is tightly linked to sanctions and rewards. Perhaps the most notable of these is the increase of *teaching to the test*. Even when the tests are improved and feature demonstrations of how students can apply their skills and knowledge in lifelike situations, the pressure to perform well on them seems to compel school personnel to rely heavily on test-prep materials, often at the expense of engaging in *real instruction*. In studies of Kentucky's assessment system, for example, researchers found that the test-related sanctions and rewards for teachers influenced them to "focus on whatever is thought to raise test scores rather than on instruction aimed at addressing individual student needs" (Jones and Whitford 1997, 277).

In other places and situations, high stakes associated with tests has created temptations for school personnel to cheat or to manipulate test results by changing the school's student population or keeping certain students out of the testing pool (Clotfeller and Ladd 1996; Darling-Hammond 1997; Smith and Rottenberg 1991). In some districts school officials are even under criminal investigation for tampering with the scores they reported for their state tests (Hoff 1999).

Fueling Racial and Class Antagonisms

This high-stakes atmosphere has also provided a backdrop for unleashing long-standing racial, ethnic, and class antagonisms that often simmer below the public surface. For example, in efforts to keep the middle class from abandoning the public schools of their racially and socioeconomically mixed districts, some school boards across the country are attempting to redraw the boundaries of school zones in a way that resegregates schools by race and class. Rather than marshalling district energies and resources to improve the quality of teaching and learning for all, these policy makers focus their efforts instead on keeping children out of their communities who are members of groups that historically have a record of scoring lower on tests.

My own community school board, I'm sad to say, is an example of this phenomenon. They recently rezoned one of the district's junior high schools, located in the most affluent and white neighborhood of the district, into a junior/senior high. In order to do this, many of the children who are bussed into the school—those who are less affluent, who are "minorities," and who are in special education—will be barred from attending. Although there has been little discussion of the teaching and learning that will go on in this school, this initiative has been presented as an effort to ensure that one particular neighborhood has a "good-quality" high school.

Teacher-Proofing Instructional Programs

In the quest for "magic bullets" to improve test scores, some schools and districts are taking a different route, returning to the "teacher-proof" solutions used in decades past. The fear of public humiliation or of losing one's job is leading principals and superintendents to resort to unusual degrees of intervention into the daily lives of teachers and students. Rather than focusing efforts on strengthening teachers' professional knowledge, administrators are enacting policies that place teachers in the role of compliant technicians who must follow the rules to produce better results. Many are requiring teachers to use standardized, highly structured curricula or to follow pacing schedules that dictate what page of the text each class should be on for each day of the school year. The Chicago Public Schools, for example, created a curriculum, introduced to schools in the fall of 1999, spelling out in detail for each day what students should be learning, what questions teachers should ask, and which parts of district and state tests each lesson addresses. It is designed to provide the superintendent with information about what the topic is in every discipline, in every grade, on any given day of the school year. On Day thirteen of the 1999–2000 school year, for example, the fourth graders were supposed to be revising writing samples while the second graders were to be practicing soft vowel sounds (Hoff 1999).

Other districts are taking similar routes. Rather than creating their own curricula, instead they are buying "Cadillac" versions of commercial texts that are accompanied by a slew of workbooks, assessment systems, and other related materials that promise to prepare students to meet state standards if only everyone buys and completes everything.

While some teachers welcome these structured curriculum plans as a helpful reference and guide, others see it as an excessive intrusion into the control of local practices. As one educator has complained:

> It's cookie-cutter curriculum. Every child's development is different and individualized. More focus should be placed on helping teachers assess where and why students have difficulties and less on test preparation. (Hoff 1999, 9)

As a result of this press to standardize teaching *inputs* in the hopes of producing better standardized *outcomes*, many educators are not only being forced to relinquish their individual teaching styles but also to pace their instruction according to district mandates rather than in response to students' needs. Some educators have even abandoned teaching practices that have been nationally recognized and recommended. Upper Arlington, Ohio is one of many districts that have dismantled integrated curricula and multiage classrooms because of the pressures from state testing. When used in these ways, many concerned educators complain that standards "put a noose on our programs" (Hoff 1999, 9).

Investing in Testing Rather Than Teacher Learning

Still another strategy that is being used in the search for higher test scores is for districts to invest their limited dollars on more testing rather than on helping teachers to become better teachers by learning how to teach in more effective ways. Some districts are adding testing at grade levels that are not covered by the state assessment system. (Coincidentally, in many places, these additional tests are produced by the same companies that produce the state exams.) During a recent school visit that I made, a teacher complained to me about the commercial test that her district was requiring her to administer to her class. It cost $250 for the class set, more than she receives to purchase classroom materials for an entire school year! Her reaction speaks to the need for investing in resources rather than tests to produce better student results:

> If this money were given to me to buy more books and materials for my students or to sponsor professional development opportunities for me and my colleagues, I could do a far better job of preparing my students for the upcoming test than more test practice will ever do.

Sometimes, as in the case above, the *more testing* approach to meeting accountability pressures comes from district or building administrators. In Texas, where the pressure of the state test is extremely strong, some principals require that their entire school devote as much as one half day a week exclusively to test practice throughout the school year. In other districts that I know of in New York

City, teachers throughout the district are directed by their principals or superintendents to spend all their instructional time in the months closest to state tests only on test-preparation activities.

But sometimes the testing practice emphasis in schools and districts is imposed from the public and their elected school board representatives. To increase the attractiveness of their districts to certain types of populations, some school boards are taking pedagogical matters into their own hands and legislating that all schools within their purview have mandated test practice throughout the school year. The school board of my own home district just passed a resolution requiring all district schools to administer five "simulation" tests during the school year to prepare students for the spring city and state standardized reading and math tests (McDermott 1999). This is in a district that is overcrowded, has many school buildings that are badly in need of repair, has high percentages of students who are English language learners, and has large numbers of inexperienced and uncertified teachers.

Relying on the Results of Only One Test as the Basis for High-Stakes Decisions

In states and districts where new external, standards-based tests are being mandated as the only acceptable measure of student and school achievement, a tragic consequence is in the making. This is a situation that is particularly poignant for me and my colleagues in New York City who have created innovative schools that have demonstrated success serving students whom the school system has previously failed. Many of these schools were the models on which standards-based reforms were created. Having redefined learning as a meaningful, purposeful enterprise, they have restructured school to match with this definition. They have utilized interdisciplinary and project-based teaching, developed authentic, performance-based ways to assess their teaching and students' learning, engaged students in community service and internships, and focused their energies and their resources on developing and deepening students' abilities to think and to help them find their place in the world.

Unfortunately, it is this kind of teaching and learning that seems to be most at risk in the new age of standards-based accountability. Particularly at the high school level, state-mandated, discipline-based graduation exams threaten to make it impossible for these schools to continue with the kind of schooling they have taken such care to develop. The press to prepare students to pass mandated exams that offer them only one way of demonstrating what they know and can do takes away from exactly the type of teaching and learning that has proven so successful with these student populations. This is especially the case with exams for disciplines like history and science, which still focus predominantly on the students' abilities to retain massive amounts of specific facts and to demonstrate their retention of these facts in only one way.

Many of these innovative, successful schools have devoted years to articulating standards—compatible with state standards—and to developing practices to realize them. Many have fully matured assessment systems that call on students to demonstrate what they know and can do in rich and variegated ways. Requiring that these schools and their students demonstrate standards in only one way negates their efforts to forge new ways for a wider range of students to experience success. Requiring only one way to demonstrate standards threatens to leave behind those who are best able to demonstrate what they know and can do in diverse or divergent ways. It threatens to leave behind those students who may not be able to pass a timed, paper and pencil test but can demonstrate a grasp of the very same standards through a project, an essay, an invention, a presentation. Why should we limit assessment so much that we must leave these students out? Why should we not allow many pathways to common goals?

We all want high standards, and of course there needs to be some kind of common assessment that can be made public. But teaching and learning is much too complex to prescribe such a uniform, easy formula as a single, sit-down, externally mandated, high-stakes test for all decisions about students' futures. We must have some flexibility in our assessment systems. We must allow for some alternative ways for students and schools to demonstrate common goals. We must not allow the standards-based movement to threaten the very existence of schools that have provided the images of possibility for reform. If we do not do this, in the name of high standards, we will, in reality, be settling for much less.

The Need for Standards for Opportunities to Learn

If we want students to learn more, why are we spending such inordinate amounts of time and money on more testing? Why are we not investing in creating incentives and supports to effectively redirect teaching practice so that it will produce more successful outcomes?

In his 1991 book, Jonathan Kozol documented the "savage inequalities" of our national educational system. He told stories of how, within the boundaries of the same district or state, some students attend schools that have state-of-the-art science laboratories, well-stocked libraries, and multimillion-dollar art facilities while others attend schools that are crumbling, overcrowded, and vastly under-resourced (Kozol 1991). These differences in learning conditions can be traced to other inequalities between and among school districts within and across states—in per-pupil expenditures, median teacher salaries, and teacher retention rates. Just within New York State, for example, per-pupil expenditures in different districts range from $5,973 to $34,623; median teacher salaries range from $29,605 to $75,206; and teacher turnover rates range from 4 percent a year to 29 percent. In some districts only 25 percent of teachers are fully certified, whereas in others 94 percent of teachers hold New York State permanent certification (New York State Education Department 1997). This situation is not dissimilar in other states across the nation where, in urban areas, there is a 30 to 40 percent vacancy rate for bilingual and English as a second language teachers; and where child poverty in cities is as high as 47 percent in Detroit, 43 percent in Atlanta, and 38 percent in Milwaukee (Tate 1994).

How does a national focus on externally mandated standards address these disparities and support better teaching and learning for all students? Depending on how standards are used, they can either help to address issues of inequity and to create school structures and practices more conducive to effective teaching and learning, or they can merely reify existing inequalities, especially for those students who have traditionally been underserved by our nation's educational system. To ensure that standards get used in helpful ways, they need to be linked to other kinds of standards—standards for opportunities to learn and standards for professional practice.

Opportunity-to-learn standards have to do with ensuring that all students have equal and adequate fiscal resources and access to well-prepared and fully qualified teachers, as well as access to high-quality curricula, instructional materials, and technologies. Many argue that high standards for all can never be achieved unless these issues are addressed (Baratz-Snowden 1993; Darling-Hammond 1991, 1993, 1994b, 1995, 1997; Darling-Hammond and Falk 1997b). Some argue even further that what is really needed to achieve high standards for all students must go far beyond attention to the educational system to include attention to all of our societal institutions—those that deal with our health and our social environments. Only such a comprehensive approach will allow all individuals to reach their potentials (Boyer 1995; Jackson 1993).

In addition to establishing standards for access to the conditions that allow learning to flourish, standards of practice are also needed to fulfill schools' responsibility to serve children well. These kinds of standards emphasize the school practices that are likely to support students' achievement of high standards: Schools that emphasize trust and respect; school and class size that allow all students to be known well; curricula that are rich and challenging; teaching that is responsive to students' cultures, needs, and understandings; and instruction that is effective in guiding, sustaining, and focusing learning in the context of clear images of excellence and the belief in the human potential to learn (Darling-Hammond 1994a, 1994b; Resnick 1987; Resnick and Hall 1998).

Opposition Grows to High-Stakes Uses of Standards and Standards-Based Tests

As more and more states put standards into effect and begin to administer high-stakes tests designed to assess whether students have met them, many parents, civil rights activists, and educators are questioning the practices being done in the name of standards. They object to the increasing standardization of the curriculum in the name of standards and to the degree that districts and states are relying on test scores for making decisions about student promotion and high school graduation. At first the opposition came mostly from political conservatives who feared federal control over local curricula. However, as state exams have increasingly been used to blame and shame students, teachers, and schools, and as many states prepare to deny students diplomas based on state exams tied to their standards, opposition has been spreading. Critics are using student boycotts, political lobbying, and lawsuits as strategies to change the penalty-oriented emphasis that is increasingly characterizing the standards movement (National Center for Fair and Open Testing 1999).

In Wisconsin, citizens are lobbying to remove funding for the development of the state's high school graduation tests. In Massachusetts, students have boycotted the state tests. In Texas, a federal lawsuit challenges the state's requirements that high school students must pass the battery of state tests in order to earn a diploma. In Virginia, high failure rates on the first administrations of the state's standards-based tests have forced the state board of education to review portions of the exam. In Oregon, the state school board has postponed implementing portions of the state test in order to provide more time to train teachers. And on the national level, charges have been issued that many state tests discriminate against students who are have limited English proficiency (Hoff 1999; White House Initiative on Educational Excellence for Hispanic Americans 1999).

Parents are often leading these opposition movements. While some are concerned about their children's futures because they may be denied high school diplomas on the basis of only one set of exams, others—who have no fear that their children will pass the tests—are concerned because they see the testing emphasis in their schools as a waste of time that could be better spent promoting more meaningful learning. These parents are unhappy that teachers are focusing their classroom time on preparing children for tests at the expense of engaging students in discussions and giving them opportunities to do research, develop experiments, and write about what they are learning. They challenge the direction standards-based reform is taking with such comments as: "In a lot of cases, our kids pass the test, but we see it as a waste of time"; or, "Essentially, these tests totally drive the curriculum" (Hoff 1999, 9).

Changing the Course of Standards-Based Reforms

Depending on how standards are shaped and used, they can either support more ambitious teaching and greater levels of success for all students, or they can serve to create higher rates of failure for those who are already least well served by the education system. Therefore it is critically important to consider carefully all of the issues that have been raised above: the substance of standards, the assessments they spawn, and the uses to which they may be put.

Students need to be the center of all our school improvement efforts, in the sense that their future is the reason for schools. Research correlating teacher effort and experience with student results clearly demonstrates that focused teaching produces learning (National Commission on Teaching and America's Future 1997). In the same way that a laser light focuses energy to produce a more powerful form of light than any other of equal energy, standards *can* help to focus teaching and to utilize energies in a more powerful way.

When students are not learning, we educators have to examine ourselves thoroughly and reflect on what we can do differently to ensure that learning does indeed take place. We have to look at and address our practices as well as the social and political factors and resources that contribute to student performance. For many students, school is the only way out of poverty (social, cultural, political, spiritual, as well as economic). They deserve our best knowledge and our intense commitment to persevere in helping them to succeed. We must be resolutely unwilling to leave any child behind.

Standards and standards-based performance assessments have the potential to help us with this challenge. But they cannot accomplish it alone. To think that simply demanding higher standards will produce better learning is "pure folly," as Susan Ohanian (1999) has charged. Ultimately raising standards for students so that they can learn what they need requires raising standards for the whole system. Only this more comprehensive view will allow us to succeed in accomplishing our goals.

Within such a comprehensive view, standards *can* be triggers for whole school, district, and state improvements. They *can* be used as a reform strategy by challenging us to answer such questions as: If all students must learn to standards, what does that mean for how we reorganize time, professional development of all staff (principals and central office staff, as well as teachers), distribution of resources, use of computers and distance learning, report cards, parent engagement,

Contrasting Ways Standards Can Be Used

Helpful Standards	Harmful Standards
Improve the quality of teaching by directing it toward worthy goals: meaningful problem solving, application of knowledge, and the pursuit of deeper understanding	Equate *harder* with *better*, without changing the quality of how things are taught, calling for "tougher" expectations that focus on acquiring "more" and "harder" skills/knowledge
Articulate core ideas and critical skills, in and across disciplines, in a way that is sufficiently pointed to be meaningful for guiding practice without being overly prescriptive	Focus on retention of prescribed, disconnected facts and skills for each discipline
Formulate "reasonable expectations" within an age span for a range of intellectual competencies and skills that children need to acquire	Require achievement of specific skills and competencies that children must acquire in order to move on to the next grade
Serve as a means for educational stakeholders to develop shared meanings and common expectations about what is considered the essentials of learning	Serve as a means for disciplinary experts to assert the importance of their respective fields by focusing on such detailed and encompassing aspects of each discipline that what a reasonable and full education entails is lost sight of and the combined expectations of all the different standards in all the different fields become humanely impossible to achieve
Are assessed through multiple standards-based performance tasks and processes that examine the degree to which students are progressing toward important ideas and skills	Are assessed through multiple-choice, norm-referenced, standardized tests that emphasize skills and facts out of the context of real-life application and that evaluate student achievement primarily in relation to the performance of other test takers
Are supported by teaching and assessments that value diverse ways of pursuing and demonstrating knowledge	Are accompanied by teaching and assessments that emphasize one "right way" and one "right answer"
Promote teaching that is responsive to how students learn, that connects to students' understandings, that guides, sustains, and focuses practice and study in the context of clear images of excellence and the potential of all to learn	Promote teaching that emphasizes conveying information and covering content and that is thought to be received better by some more than by others because intelligence is inherently "fixed"
Use assessment results as one of many sources of evidence to inform instruction, to keep students and parents apprised of progress, to trigger special supports for students who need them, to analyze how teaching practices can be improved, and to make decisions about where resources should be allocated	Use assessment results as the sole basis for making decisions about what group or track students should be placed in, whether students should be promoted or retained in grade, whether students should graduate from school
Are accompanied by standards for the opportunities to learn—standards of access and standards of practice—that are needed for all to achieve desired goals	Focus exclusively on content and performance standards for students with little attention directed at addressing the broader contexts that enable or prohibit school improvement efforts

Figure 5–1

press coverage of education, state legislation, teacher preparation and licensure, and postsecondary education?

All these aspects of schooling and more must be subjected to one basic question: Does the way we are conducting our lives in school now help us get to the heart of the matter—powerful teaching and powerful learning for all students in our schools? If the answer is no, then we must think of ways to redesign how we conduct our school lives so that we focus on these essential matters.

Standards and standards-based assessments will not ultimately support better learning if they are used simply to allocate rewards and sanctions, determine automatic grade retentions, or withhold diplomas. Neither will standards support better learning if they are measured by only one test. No one test should ever determine whether a student has met the school's, district's, state's, or even the student's personal learning goals. A combination of assessments should be collected to demonstrate students' accomplishments. Students should have time as well as multiple opportunities to take exams before the end of their school years so that they and their teachers can see where more work is needed and mobilize the appropriate supports.

Standards and standards-based assessments *can* ultimately support better learning if they are used to direct teaching toward worthy goals, to promote teaching that is responsive to how students learn, to examine students in multiple ways that can be used to inform instruction, to keep students and parents apprised of progress, to trigger special supports for students who need them, and to evaluate school practices. If all these aspects of the standards, assessment, and accountability picture are addressed, standards and standards-based assessments have the potential to be of enormous benefit to teaching and learning.

Chapter 6

Using Standards and Assessments to Support Teaching and Learning

The theoretical arguments have been made: Standards and related assessments can be useful or harmful—depending on how they are developed and used. Other issues and questions arise: What does a helpful approach to standards and assessments actually look like in practice? How are teachers or school principals supposed to translate the often massive standards documents that they receive from district or state education department offices into curricula that explores exciting ideas, connects to students' interests, pursues genuine understanding, and results in powerful learning? How can curricular coherence be created among classrooms on a grade level and across grade levels in a school without mandating what teachers teach, how they teach it, and the ways in which students are going to learn?

This chapter explores these questions, how they can be tackled in the classroom as well as throughout a grade and across an entire school. It suggests ways to connect standards, assessment, curriculum, and instruction; ways that enable teachers to simultaneously (1) help all students learn important ideas, skills, and knowledge, and (2) utilize evidence of students' learning so teaching can be shaped in light of those understandings. Two processes are presented—for the whole school and for the classroom teacher—to focus attention on understanding what students understand and on how to use that understanding as a guide to teaching. These processes are not intended to be a prescription, recipe, or program that casts teaching merely as delivering inputs and measuring outcomes only *after the fact* of teaching. In these processes, assessment is at the *center* of the teaching/learning process.

Keeping the Learner at the Center of Curriculum

Cognitive research and successful practices inform us that powerful learning occurs when teachers create opportunities for learners to construct their own understandings through active involvement with ideas, materials, and relationships, and when teachers provide occasions for learners to explore, question, hypothesize, and argue about ideas with others. The effective teacher pays careful attention to the information contained within learners' responses, questions, conjectures, and comments to each particular learning experience. The effective teacher then uses this information to shape instruction, all the while carefully scaffolding the cognitive mix with more questions, suggestions, information, and skills until new levels of complexity have been mastered and others begin to form on the horizon. Such a teacher is a guide to new terrains of knowledge, hovering nearby like a nurturing parent, to assist, provoke, encourage, and provide the safety needed for the risk-taking of genuine learning to occur.

Keeping this image of learning in mind as we work with standards to develop curriculum is a potent reminder that our teaching task is not merely about *covering* the standards. Learning does not occur simply by mapping curriculum to standards and then performing specified teaching activities. Only when we affect significant changes in our students' understandings do we know that learning has occurred. Our teaching task then is to find ways to *uncover* the important issues and ideas of the world expressed by standards and, most importantly, to ensure that students understand these ideas, make sense of them, and ultimately come to own them in their own ways. We thus need to ensure that our teaching practices include not only our intentions about how to reach our goals but also our plans of what we will look for as evidence that our students have learned (Tyler 1949).

Curriculum is often constructed under the assumption that learners have no impact on our plans. This current epoch's emphasis on standards and accountability is ironically increasing the frequency of this phenomenon. Curricula are often designed and mandated to be impervious to the learners who are involved. From many schools and district offices, directives are being issued for teachers to deliver curriculum and instruction on a schedule—short vowel sounds on the first Monday of October, place value on the third Thursday of November. Inevitable real-life interruptions—fire drills, sicknesses, holidays, world events—are not supposed to be considered; teachable moments are not to be taken advantage of; different paces and styles of learning are supposed to be ignored.

But students do not necessarily learn on such timetables or in response to such methods. To persist as if they do and to demand that they will is simply "magical thinking" (Fraiberg 1959). Such an approach to standards and curriculum can lead only to certain and repeated failure. We cannot help children to learn if we are not responsive to what they know and can do. We cannot support children's development if we are not also sensitive and attentive to their struggles and misunderstandings, to their emerging interests and epiphanies, to their unanticipatable difficulties and detours. If we are to help learners to learn, we must allow them to impact the curriculum and its outcomes.

To teach effectively is thus to be faced with an intractable tension: There are certain things that students can and need to be expected to learn and to learn to do but, in order to support them in their learning, we must consider their needs, adjust to their understandings, and adapt to their idiosyncrasies. If we continue teaching the planned curriculum as if nothing is happening on the part of the learner, out of fear that we will lose sight of our goals, we risk encountering a far greater and ultimately more tragic problem—losing the learner and leaving him behind.

Curriculum and instruction plans need to be more like maps of important sites on a journey than travel itineraries that schedule places and activities for each hour of each day. Teachers need conceptual guides to important knowledge and skills, accompanied by sufficient detail about the significant strategies and behaviors students need to master in the course of their learning journeys. But no guide, plan, or syllabus can effectively script how and at what pace learners will learn. No guide can anticipate the surprises and difficulties that will arise. Neither can it predict in advance the fullness of the learning that will take place. And certainly no guide can guarantee that material will be learned just because it has been presented.

> A syllabus organized around knowledge and skills to be covered can never provide a criterion for learner success or safeguard against ineffective and (from the students' viewpoint) aimless teaching. (Wiggins 1998, 224)

Using Evidence to Guide Teaching

Throughout the course of our teaching we have to consider not only our curriculum and lesson plans but also their impact on our students. Only when we build into our plans a way to take into account what is happening with our students—through a continual gathering of evidence of what they understand and how they can actually apply their understandings—will we have a way to assess the effectiveness of our plans, to make adjustments to our teaching, and to heighten the likelihood that learning will occur.

This is why performance tasks and other kinds of authentic assessments are so helpful and central to effective teaching. The knowledge we gain of what students know from the evidence we collect with authentic assessments can be an invaluable guide to our instruction. It gives us clues to what we need to do to help our students gain mastery of skills and to ensure that they understand important concepts. It offers us insights about each student's unique way of processing information, of approaching and making sense of the world. And it prevents us, when students have difficulties with their learning, from attributing these difficulties to some flaw in their intellect or their character. Rather, it focuses us on *our* responsibility to try to understand students' thinking, their issues and their problems; to keep searching for the keys to their learning until we can find ways to help them succeed (Elbow 1986).

Learning Is a Process

This way of thinking about the centrality of assessment to curriculum and teaching is also connected to the conception that learning is a process—a process of trial and error toward mastery and understanding. Jerome Bruner (1960) referred to this process as one that is interactive and that moves in spiraling rather than linear ways. It is a process that requires repeated opportunities to directly experience ideas by engaging in the production of work that stems from those ideas (Dewey 1916).

> From the outset of education and all along the way, the learner should be given the chance to solve problems, to conjecture, to quarrel as these are done at the heart of a discipline. (Bruner 1960, 230)

As ideas are continually revisited and as problems and issues that arise from putting these ideas into use are repeatedly experienced, insights and understandings are continually deepened.

By reshaping and reordering knowledge through action, reflection, reconsideration, and revision, students come to understand and master what they are learning; they learn to produce their own understandings, not just the results of others' thinking. They learn to arrive at results and to create new ideas themselves. Eleanor Duckworth calls this "the having of wonderful ideas" (Duckworth 1987). Anyone who has experienced this knows how truly wonderful it can be. Anyone who has helped someone to really understand or invent an idea knows that this is the stuff that makes teaching such an incredibly rewarding experience.

Teaching for Understanding

The teaching task, then, is to construct experiences that bring students in contact with important issues and ideas. These experiences should raise problems that arise as the ideas are applied in real-life situations. The goal is the production, use, and extension of knowledge. The challenge is to organize the experiences in such a way that each one emerges from the ones prior. The aim is to organize a set of experiences for the learner that produces a coherent understanding of the whole.

In doing this, a balance must be struck between predetermined goals and the learners' interests and understandings. The curriculum and its flow cannot be derived solely from what students may like at the moment or from what a linear plan for coverage may suggest. Rather, curriculum must flow from an interplay among the standards, goals, and purposes of the teacher's plan and the feedback that is obtained from the learner in the course of putting new knowledge and skills to use. This feedback needs to continually drive the further development of the plan.

The process is deliberate and logical. It is driven by the evidence that teachers gather about their learners—how they demonstrate their grasp of the key ideas, competencies, and understandings embodied in any study. Various frameworks for this process have been created to guide the work of classrooms and schools (Harris and Carr 1996; Stiggins 1997; Wiggins and McTighe 1998). What all of these frameworks share is a belief that ongoing feedback from the learner and ongoing adjustment to teaching based on this feedback is at the heart of all learning.

Building Coherence of Purpose and Practice in a School

The framework in Figure 6–1 presents a process for how to engage educators throughout a school in developing a whole school curriculum and assessment plan. Each question can be a starting point for schoolwide reflection, discussion, and planning at faculty meetings or school retreats. When worked on in concert with other colleagues, these questions can help educators in a school create the unity of purpose and action that is a hallmark of a coherent learning community.

Group brainstorming, as a whole school or by grade level, can be useful for the problem solving needed to address the questions of this framework. Figure 6–2 illustrates how one school community, the Muscota New School in New York City's Community School District 6, addressed the first question. To create this chart, the Muscota New School faculty articulated their own goals and purposes, connecting them with their state standards. By referencing examples from their practice, they began to put flesh on the skeleton of the standards.

The ideas shown here, generated some years ago at a whole school retreat, are just about literacy. They are part of a larger document that includes all the disciplines.

After articulating their goals, the Muscota New School faculty moved on to

Schoolwide Process for Using Standards and Assessments to Build Coherence in a School

Step I: Getting Clear About Standards
1. What are your *goals, purposes, and expectations* for students?

   What are the core ideas—the most important and enduring issues, principles, concepts—in and across the various disciplines?

   What are the critical skills for each discipline?

   What are the key dispositions or habits of mind across all disciplines?

2. What are the *learning goals of your students and their families*, obtained through parents' meetings, teacher-family conferences?
3. How do you *connect these goals to each other and to the standards* articulated by professional organizations and your state/district?

Step II: Setting Standards for Performance
4. What are *reasonable expectations for students to accomplish in relation to your goals/ standards*?

   At what stages of development or by what grade? (For example, What do you want students to know and be able to do by the time they graduate? By what other junctures in their schooling?)

Step III: Determining What and How to Teach
5. What kinds of *learning experiences and activities* will have the power to engage students and to stimulate and support learning in relation to these standards?

Step IV: Assessing Student Progress
6. What *evidence of student learning* will you collect to give you an indication of how students are progressing toward the goals/standards?

   What ongoing (formative) assessments will you use to inquire about and keep track of *how* students are progressing?

   What evaluation (summative) assessments will you use to determine *what* students have learned?

   What process is in place to elicit students' and families' perspectives on students' progress?

   Are there assessments that you as a community want everyone to do at certain times in a student's life in school? If so, what do you want them to be (i.e., reading sample, research report, math project, etc.)? When do you want them to be done (i.e., by the end of third grade, the end of fifth grade, middle school, high school?)

7. How will you share this information among your faculty and with the families and community of your school)?

Step V: Ensuring Opportunities to Learn
8. What *materials, resources, and supports* (from the school, district, state) do you need to accomplish your goals?
9. What *resources and supports* will you provide to students who do not meet the goals and standards within reasonable timetable expectations?

Figure 6–1   ©2000 by Beverly Falk from *The Heart of the Matter*, Portsmouth, NH: Heinemann

Muscota New School's Literacy Goals and Values

Goal/Value	*Classroom Example*
Multiple literacies and languages	Doing/seeing as literacy: movement/dance, music, cooking, math, art, building, living with multiple languages
Read fluently and comprehend	Newspapers, recipes, information from a variety of sources and different kinds of literature
Articulate thoughts and ideas	Brainstorming, writing, sharing, editing, publishing
Communicate effectively	Writing, speaking
Literary expression	Story writing, poetry
Public speaking	Sharing at town meeting; kids as school tour guides
Be able to use the appropriate conventions of the language	Knowledge of contractions, homonyms, adjectives, etc.
Vocabulary	Using and defining words specific to a content area; encouraging vocabulary development in writing and discussion
Presentation of work	Revising/editing

Figure 6–2

create the chart in Figure 6–3, which illustrates the progression of the faculty's discussion to Questions 3 and 5 of the framework in Figure 6–1. Here they listed the learning opportunities provided in their classrooms and how these opportunities incorporate the essential knowledge and skills expressed in the state standards.

The Muscota New School faculty worked on connecting what they teach to their goals and the standards by beginning with the practices they already had in place, assessing what gaps, if any, existed, and adding to their program based on that assessment.

Another way to develop a standards-based approach to teaching is to generate new topics or themes of study that incorporate the ideas and skills of different

Muscota New School's Practices to Support Progress Toward the State Learning Standards for the English Language

Practice	Standard 1 Information and Understanding	Standard 2 Literary Response and Expression	Standard 3 Critical Analysis and Evaluation	Standard 4 Social Interaction
Morning message	●		●	●
Meetings/sharings writers workshop math congress readers workshop morning meetings process meetings community	●	●	●	●
Readers workshop quiet reading reading groups read alouds Reading games Shared reading big books guided reading Genre studies Author studies Response journals	●	●	●	●
Songs conventions of print word families receive and use info	●	●	●	●
Poetry	●	●	●	●
Research groups documenting surveys interviews	●		●	●

Book making	●	●	●	●
Library trips/use	●	●	●	●
Writing newsletters/papers conferences journals reflection response process (editing/revising) labeling/signs letters e-mail recipes	●	●	●	●
Drama plays/puppet shows	●	●	●	●
Debates	●	●		●
Maps	●	●		●
Tour guides	●	●		●
Problem solving	●	●		●
Exhibitions/museums	●	●		●
Mentoring	●	●		●
Festivals/celebrations	●	●		●

Figure 6–3

standards. Figure 6–4 is an example of this approach. It illustrates how the teachers at the Lillian Weber School, P.S. 84 in New York City's Community School District 3, developed a menu of studies for each grade level that embodies their state's science and social studies standards. The faculty agreed to choose from this menu when deciding each year what to study in their classrooms so that students would have continuity as they move from grade to grade within the school. Decisions about what studies should take place in different grades were made by considering several factors: themes and issues appropriate for different stages of development, how knowledge and skills build on each other over the years, and the state standards.

Making the decision to strive for this kind of curricular coherence across a school has its benefits and its problems. By committing to specific studies, teachers limit their freedom somewhat to build curriculum that is centered on being responsive to their own and their students' interests. What is gained from this way of working, however, is curricular coherence across the school. A pathway for learning can be identified for students during their time in the school. In addition, knowing in advance some of the studies they will be doing gives teachers time to scout out resources and to plan engaging activities and trips to enhance the learning. Teachers can share ideas with colleagues and work out ways for students across classes to work together. Although this way of working requires committing to the study of several topics in advance, the learning that takes place in the classroom need not be limited only to the agreed-upon curricula. There still can be room for taking advantage of the "teachable moment" and for engaging in other inquiries that emerge from the interests of the students.

In all aspects of our lives we deal with tensions between individual and community needs. We all need space to express our unique selves, to follow our interests, and to work in our own ways. But we also need to find ways to balance all this with the fact that we are part of a larger community. In schools, we need some common experiences, knowledge, language, and meanings in order to do what is best for the children. Standards-based work offers us a way to build such commonalities together.

To develop a whole school curriculum and assessment framework may take as long as one year, or even two. Engaging in the development process, however, is a powerful learning experience that helps to clarify and articulate beliefs and practices. The result is that participants gain clearer understandings about what they do, why they do what they do, and how practices fit into a whole. The entire school community is strengthened as a result. An image of the flamingo comes to mind: When preparing to fly, flamingos rise slowly. Once aloft, however, they begin to soar. And then they are truly a magnificent sight.*

---

*I owe this metaphor to my colleague, Alicia Thomas, an extraordinary educational leader from the Northeast Independent School District in San Antonio, Texas.

P.S. 84's Menu of Social Studies and Science Studies

	Grade		Investigations
		Class A	Pet Store; Myself
	K	Class B	Pet Store; Myself
		Class C	Pet Store; Myself
		Class D	Pet Store; Myself
		Class A	Bakery; Living things; Neighborhood; Balls and Ramps
	1	Class B	Bakery; Living Things; Neighborhood; Balls and Ramps
		Class C	Bakery; Living Things; Neighborhood; Air and Weather
		Class A	Market; Living Things; Post Office; Sand and Silt
		Class B	Market; Living Things; Post Office; Balls and Ramps
	1/2	Class C	Market; Living Things; Post Office; Balls and Ramps
		Class D	Market; Living Things; Post Office; Balls and Ramps
		Class A	Market; Growing Things; Clothing; Sand and Silt
	2	Class B	Market; Growing Things; Clothing; Sand and Silt

Grade	Class	Social Studies Investigations	Science Investigations
2/3	Class A	Mexico; China	Growing Things; Liquids
	Class A	Serengeti Plains; Puerto Rico	Animal Habitats; Sound
	Class B	Mexico; China	Animal Habitats; Sound
3	Class C	Puerto Rico; Inuit	Animal Habitats; Sound
	Class D	Japan; Mexico	Animal Habitats; Sound
	Class E	Congo; India	Animal Habitats; Sound
	Class A	Immigration	Bones & Skeletons; Circuits
4	Class B	Early Explorers	Bones & Skeletons; Circuits
	Class C	Native Americans; Colonial New York	Bones & Skeletons; Circuits
4/5	Class A	Amazon River Basin; Inuit	Animal Adaptations; Air and Water
	Class B	Africa; U. S. History	Growing Things; Circuits
	Class A	Caribbean; U. S. History	Human Body; Land Forms; Marine Biology
5	Class B	U. S. History; Mexico	Human Body; Land Forms
	Class C	Mayan; U. S. History	Human Body; Land Forms

Figure 6–4

Creating Standards-Based Curriculum and Assessment in the Classroom

In keeping with the process described above for creating curricular coherence across a whole school, the framework in Figure 6–5 is a process that individual teachers can use to develop their classroom curriculum and instructional plans. The process of developing this curriculum can begin either with standards or simply with an idea, a question, or even a wondering. It can be used to formulate new plans or simply to articulate existing plans so that the goals and standards inherent in them are made more explicit for all to understand.

Classroom Process for Using Standards and Assessments to Create a Curriculum Plan

---

Step I: Framing the Question

What is the topic or theme of this study? Organize the study around a major understanding, problem, issue, or question. It should be broad enough to include several standards, relevant to students' lives and interests, suitable to students' ages and abilities, and sensitive to racial and cultural biases. It should include multiple ways for students to learn and to express their understandings. One way to engage and motivate students is to have them brainstorm questions they have about the world. Identify commonalties from these questions that can be organized into a group study.

Step II: Identifying the Standards/Goals of the Study

Think about:

Core Ideas   What concepts and knowledge does this study help students explore, assimilate, and apply?

Critical Skills   What skills in language arts, mathematics, the arts, etc. will children acquire or practice in the course of this study?

Key Dispositions and Habits of Mind   What ways of learning, of providing evidence for assertions, of developing relationships with others, will this study provide opportunities to develop?

Step III: Formulating Key Questions

What are key questions that can guide the study? With your students, brainstorm questions (about ten) that you all wonder about related to the study. Develop some overarching questions that incorporate these more specific questions.

Step IV: Creating Learning Activities

What are the *experiences, activities, projects, experiments*, etc. that will help students examine the concepts, learn the skills, and develop the dispositions that this study intends to nurture?

Figure 6–5   ©2000 by Beverly Falk from *The Heart of the Matter*. Portsmouth, NH: Heinemann

How can these activities be planned and sequenced to stimulate students' interest, build students' knowledge and skills, and provide opportunities for students to demonstrate what they are learning?

What resources—books, materials, technology, etc.—are needed to support the work of this study?

What out-of-school activities can enrich the learning of the study?

What cross-grade/age experiences can support the study? What activity that is of service to others can be incorporated into this study?

What homework assignments can support the study? How can parents/families be involved?

Step V: Reviewing Your Plans

Review the activities of the study for what standards and what disciplines are involved. Is there anything that you wanted to include that you left out? If so, how can you incorporate it in the study? Making a grid, like the one below, can be helpful in keeping track of and sharing this information.

Activity	Lang. Arts	Math	Social Studies	Science	The Arts	Physical Ed.
Activity 1	X		X		X	
Activity 2		X		X		
Activity 3	X	X	X			
Activity 4		X				X

Step VI: Assessing Student Learning

What tasks, performances, and/or products will demonstrate students' learning during this study?

What will you do to assess student progress along the way (formative assessment)?

How will you use what you learn from the formative assessments to shape and guide the rest of the study?

What culminating experience will students do to assess the degree to which they have achieved the goals of the study (summative assessment)?

What are the criteria for performance (based on the standards) that can guide students as they engage in the assessment activities for the study?

What does accomplished work look like for each task? Describe what each criterion for the task would look like in the most accomplished work. Then describe how the criterion would appear at different levels of performance. (This is the scoring guide or rubric.)

What samples of student work illustrate the different performance levels described in the rubric? These are called benchmarks.

Figure 6–5 (Continued)   ©2000 by Beverly Falk from *The Heart of the Matter*. Portsmouth. NH: Heinemann

Use a Variety of Assessments Throughout Your Study

As you proceed through your study, use specific performance tasks or other kinds of assessments (as discussed in Chapter 3) to give you information about how your students are progressing. Do not wait for the culminating project of the study to do your assessment of students' learning. Check in with students regularly throughout the study so that you can shape instructions more effectively, nip problems in the bud, make sure no one falls through the cracks. My colleague, Linda Margolin, does this as she conducts individual research studies with her fourth-grade class. In addition to collecting their ongoing assignments, at the conclusion of daily research work sessions she frequently asks her students to answer a set of questions to help her keep track of how they are progressing:

> What did you work on in your research today?
> What did you notice about what you were doing?
> What problems did you have? Where did you get stuck?
> What is your plan for what to do next?
> Tell me something you want me to know about you.

Linda reviews the responses to these questions to help her respond to her students' questions, to develop minilessons that address her students' needs, and to plan individual assistance or intervention for students who may be floundering. Not only do students' responses provide Linda with information about what skills and concepts she needs to help strengthen, they also give her invaluable insight into her students' attitudes and approaches to learning. For example, Neshawn's response to Linda's questions reveals a lot about his view of himself as a learner:

> I noticed that it was a lot of work trying to find my big question. I noticed that I like working hard.

Tasks and Rubrics Offer Guidance to Learning

In addition to including ongoing, informal feedback throughout the course of a study, standards-based performance assessment tasks that have clear criteria and rubrics can also be included in a study to help guide students to develop and demonstrate the skills you are seeking to help them develop. Figure 6–6 illustrates a task designed to assess the language arts standard "Listening for Information and Understanding Task." Note how the task clearly describes the criteria for what needs to be done. Note how the rubric describes qualities of the work that take into account the task criteria and reflect the standard for different levels of performance.

Remember to include different kinds of tasks in your study to ensure that students who have different modes of learning will have an opportunity to demonstrate their learning through their strengths. Wherever possible, include several assessment options to put into practice the findings of research on motivation, multiple intelligences, and learning styles that students produce better work when they have some choice in determining what they do. For example, in addition to a required written research report, also require students to do something else to demonstrate what they have learned. Let them choose from among

Listening for Information and Understanding Task

DIRECTIONS: Write a report using the situation given below and information from the speech you have just heard. You may use your notes to plan your writing.

Cynthia Rylant's speech could be described as a celebration of the people and events that have influenced her development as a writer of books for young people. Write a report for your class in which you discuss the people and experiences Rylant celebrates in her speech. In what ways have those people and experiences influenced her as a writer?

In your report, be sure to:

- Identify the people and experiences that influenced Rylant's development as a writer
- Describe the ways in which those people and experiences influenced her development as a writer
- Support your discussion with specific evidence from the speech
- Provide information from the speech that is accurate, relevant, and complete
- Organize your report in a logical and coherent manner
- Use correct grammar, spelling, and punctuation

Figure 6–6   ©2000 by Beverly Falk from *The Heart of the Matter*, Portsmouth, NH: Heinemann

such options as artwork, a video or computer presentation, a skit or other type of performance.

Scoring guides or rubrics that accompany performance tasks such as the one used to assess the Listening for Information and Understanding Task illustrated in Figure 6–7 on pp. 120–121 are made up of criteria that are based on the standards, a scale, and performance descriptions. These elements are put together in different ways, depending on the purpose for which the rubric will be used. Rubrics can have full descriptions for each level of performance (as in Figure 6–7) or they can use only numbers to indicate to what degree the work approaches or meets a described standard (see Figure 6–8 on page 122).

Rubrics can be holistic or analytic. They can be used for general or task-specific purposes. Holistic rubrics give overall descriptions of work that translate into a single score. Familiar examples of holistic rubrics are those used in Advanced Placement Examinations and in some sports competitions such as diving. The math task in Figure 4–2 is an example of a holistic rubric.

In contrast, analytic rubrics offer separate descriptions for the different criteria of a task. Each criterion is scored and then these scores get added up to produce one overall score that evaluates the entire performance. Different criteria are sometimes given more weight than others based on their importance. An example of this kind of scoring is a skating competition, which usually evaluates skaters by combining separate scores for technical and artistic merit. This way of assessing performance is useful in clarifying expectations for different aspects of a task or performance. The scoring guide in Figure 6–8 is an example of an analytic rubric.

Rubrics can be used for different purposes. This too is reflected in their design. They can be developed either to assess a specific task or to assess many tasks that represent a skill or body of knowledge. A task-specific rubric or scoring guide is useful for evaluating how a student has met the unique criteria that are specified for a particular task. The scoring guide in Figure 6–8 is a task-specific rubric. It is useful only for that task and cannot be used to monitor student progress over time or across several different tasks. In contrast, a general rubric or scoring guide describes criteria or qualities for a more generic activity, such as reading. The Reading Scale in Figure 4–9 is a generic scale that can be used to monitor general progress in reading over time, across several pieces of work, using multiple products and performances.

Student Work Samples Bring Standards to Life

What really brings descriptions of standards to life are samples of student work that exemplify how the criteria of standards-based work are met at different levels of performance. Student work samples ground the descriptions of a rubric's criteria in concrete examples. In this way they serve as stable reference points for what scores mean across student work over time. Samples of student work also offer students a vision of possibility of what to aim for. By demonstrating, in advance, how work will be evaluated, work samples, in conjunction with rubrics, can guide students as they proceed in their learning. Because they clarify the expectations of the standards in concrete and meaningful ways, work samples are also effective at communicating the substance of standards to parents and other interested parties.

Reliability and Validity

When developing tasks and rubrics it is important to take care that realistic expectations guide the work. In formulating these expectations, it is important to consider long-range goals as well as what is developmentally appropriate and feasible to attain. Otherwise, standards may be set in such a way that disproportionate numbers of students fail to meet them. This was the case recently in Virginia, where well over 90 percent of the students did not meet the standards set by the state exams. Did the students fail because students, teachers, and schools have been doing such a poor job at teaching and learning, or is there something unreasonable about the difficulty level of what students are being asked to do on the exams? Careful consideration must be paid to these questions when crafting any standards and standards-based assessments. How these questions are addressed affects how valid and reliable any standards and assessments will be.

A useful way to ensure that any standards-based study, project, or assessment task is valid and maintains an appropriate balance between rigorous standards and reasonable expectations is to develop the work by continually cross-referencing expectations with student work. It is also helpful to bear in mind what learning theory tells us students can and should be able to do. After the goals and expectations are set, it is important to gather student work and review it for how it meets initial expectations. This evidence can then be used to help determine how reasonable the initial expectations are. Questions need to be asked, such as: What expectations in the work do students seem unable to do? Are they unable to do it because we haven't taught it to them, we haven't taught it to them properly, or it is an inappropriate expectation at this point in students' development?

These questions need to be asked when formulating expectations as well as when creating work plans and assessments. The development process for

Rubric for Listening for Information and Understanding Task

SCORING RUBRIC

QUALITY	5 The response:	4 The response:	3 The response:	2 The response:	1 The response:
Meaning: *the extent to which the response:* • *accurately identifies the people and experiences that influenced Rylant's development as a writer* • *interprets and analyzes the impact of those people and experiences on Rylant's development as a writer*	• Conveys a clear, full, and accurate description of the people and experiences that influenced Rylant's development as a writer • Goes beyond the factual information presented to interpret and analyze the impact of those people and experiences on Rylant's development as a writer	• Conveys a clear, full, and accurate, though not necessarily complete, description of the people and experiences that influenced Rylant's development as a writer • Makes connections and presents some analysis and interpretation of the impact of those people and experiences on Rylant's development as a writer	• Conveys an accurate, but not necessarily complete, description of the people or experiences that influenced Rylant's development as a writer • Makes some connections between people and experiences and their impact	• Identifies some of the people or experiences that influenced Rylant's development as a writer • Makes irrelevant or few connections between people or experiences and their impact	• Conveys a sketchy or inaccurate summary of the speech • Makes no connections between people or experiences and their impact
Development: *the extent to which the discussion is elaborated through the use of specific, accurate, and relevant ideas and information from the speech*	• Develops and elaborates discussion clearly and fully, using a wide range of specific, accurate, and relevant ideas and information from the speech • Anticipates audience response in selecting and using information from the speech	• Develops discussion clearly, using specific, accurate, and relevant ideas and information from the speech	• Develops ideas simply, using some details from the speech	• Includes few supporting details, with ideas largely undeveloped. May include inaccurate or irrelevant information	• Conveys vague or unsupported ideas, or presents random information and details unrelated to the topic

120

Criteria					
Organization: the extent to which the response exhibits direction, shape, and coherence	• Establishes a clear, original, and relevant context and focus for the report • Exhibits a logical and coherent organizational structure through effective use of such devices as an introduction, conclusion, and transitions that contribute to the cohesion of the whole	• Establishes a clear and relevant context and focus for the report • Exhibits a logical and coherent organizational structure through the use of such devices as an introduction, conclusion, and transitions	• Establishes an appropriate context for the report • Exhibits a discernible structure	• Establishes some direction for the report, but organization is tentative	• Lacks context or focus for the report • Shows little or no evidence of organization
Language Use: The extent to which the response exhibits effective use of words, sentence structure, and sentence variety to convey ideas and information to a given audience	• Conveys ideas and information in original and precise language, with a noticeable sense of voice and awareness of audience • Makes effective use of sentence structure and length to convey ideas	• Conveys ideas and information in original and precise language, with some awareness of audience • Shows consistent use of sentences that are varied in length and structure	• Uses language from the speech to convey ideas and information • Relies on sentences that are unvaried in length and structure	• Relies on ordinary, often imprecise, language to convey information • Relies on sentences that lack variety in structure and length and may be constructed incorrectly	• Includes vague, inappropriate, and/or incorrect language • Relies on run-ons or sentence fragments
Conventions: the extent to which the response exhibits conventional spelling, punctuation, paragraphing, grammar, and usage	• Exhibits correct spelling, punctuation, paragraphing, grammar, and usage	• Exhibits generally correct spelling, punctuation, paragraphing, grammar, and usage	• Exhibits minor errors in spelling, punctuation, paragraphing, grammar, or usage that do not interfere with communication	• Exhibits errors in spelling, punctuation, paragraphing, grammar, or usage that may interfere with communication	• Exhibits errors in spelling, punctuation, paragraphing, grammar, or usage that often interfere with communication

Figure 6–7

©2000 by Beverly Falk from *The Heart of the Matter*. Portsmouth, NH: Heinemann

Research Article Analysis Task and Rubric

Complete a three- to five-page paper that reviews/analyzes an article that is related to your research interest. Using the criteria for research we have discussed in class, please address the following questions:

1. What is the research question addressed by this study?
2. Discuss the methodology of this study:
   a. What type of research produced this study (qualitative or quantitative or both)? Please explain with examples of how the research embodies the characteristics of its type.
   b. Discuss the perspective of the researcher, his/her background, assumptions, biases.
   c. What sources of data were used to address the research questions (i.e., observations, surveys, interviews, etc.)?
   d. Who collected the data?
   e. How and when was the data collected?
3. What does the author conclude as a result of this research? How are the assertions in the author's analysis backed up by evidence?
4. What do *you* think about the conclusions of this study? Do you agree/disagree? Do you think that the author has misinterpreted, ignored, underemphasized or overemphasized particular aspects of the research question(s)?
5. What questions are you left with after reading this study?

Grading Criteria for Research Article Analysis

0—not achieved   3—partially achieved   5—fully achieved

Your work will be graded according to the extent to which your paper incorporates the following criteria:

- Addresses all the guiding questions   _____
- Makes connections between ideas discussed in class and
  in the readings   _____
- Uses evidence from the research article being reviewed
  to support ideas and analysis   _____
- Communicates ideas clearly and in a well-organized
  manner   _____

TOTAL SCORE: _____

Figure 6–8   ©2000 by Beverly Falk from *The Heart of the Matter*. Portsmouth, NH: Heinemann standards-based curriculum and assessment needs to work back and forth among standards, criteria, descriptions of performance, and student work (see Figure 6–9).

Working in this way will help to ensure that our expectations, as expressed in our standards, our curriculum, and our assessment, are authentic and valid reflections of what students actually can do.

Reliability is also an important issue to address when developing standards-based assessments. A reliable assessment will provide a consistent view of student work. That means if different people look at the work, they will evaluate it in a similar way. It also means that work completed by the same person at different times will be evaluated similarly by the assessment.

As discussed in earlier chapters, assessment reliability and validity are particularly difficult to achieve with performance tasks that are to be used to influence decisions that involve high-stakes consequences such as graduation, retention, or promotion. However, when developing assessments that are going to be used in

Developing Rubrics for Standards-Based Assessments

Articulate standards that the task is assessing.

↓

Spell out criteria for the task.

↓

Describe performance for each criterion at different levels of performance.

↓

EVALUATE/SCORE STUDENT WORK.

↑

Describe how student work meets task criteria.

↑

Examine student work.

↑

Gather student work.

Figure 6–9   ©2000 by Beverly Falk from *The Heart of the Matter*, Portsmouth, NH: Heinemann

the classroom primarily for instructional purposes, reasonable reliability can be reached by making sure that the assessment provides:

- Criteria that are clear, do not overlap, and are specifically linked to standards. (Make sure not to confuse *criteria* with *expectations* for how products and performances are to be produced. Examples of criteria that relate to standards are "using details to support ideas" or "making connections." Examples of expectations for how a product is to be produced are "the paper must be typed" or "the paper should be 1000 words.")
- Scales that make clear distinctions between levels
- Performance descriptions that are specific, observable, and can be documented
- Exemplars of student work that illustrate levels of performance
- Evidence that the judgments of those who are assessing can be consistent over time and across students and assessors (Harris and Carr 1996)

The amazing thing about working with standards-based assessments is that, over time, they stimulate teachers and students to develop common understandings and expectations about what constitutes quality work. Teachers start to develop shared meanings and a common language that provides consistency and coherence across the school. Students get clearer images of expectations and become more adept at monitoring their own learning. The clearer the standards, the better-guided students are to reach them, and the higher the quality of work that is ultimately produced. So, in effect, standards-based work, by its very nature, leads to the development of higher standards.

Using Standards to Communicate About Learning

By consciously building standards into curriculum plans and assessment tasks and by explicitly gathering evidence of how standards are met, teachers, students, and their families gain a clear sense of what students know and can do. They get to see how students are progressing in relation to the standards, to other students, and, most importantly, to themselves.

Report Cards

Many school communities are finding that, as they switch to a standards-based approach to their work, old ways of reporting student progress are no longer useful or make sense. Many school communities working in standards-based ways are creating new report cards that describe student progress in relation to standards instead of relying on letter grades or evaluations such as *excellent, good, fair,* or *poor.* This excerpt from the report card at the Lillian Weber School, P.S. 84, is an example of a beginning effort to develop a standards-based report card (Figure 6–10).

Other examples of standards-based reporting are associated with use of *The Early Literacy Profile,* discussed in Chapter 4. Its reading scale (see Figure 4–9) reports students' literacy progress along a continuum of eight stages. A number of schools and districts using the ELP are transforming their reporting systems to reflect the core knowledge, skills, and dispositions described in *The Early Literacy Profile* scales. Evaluations of individual students are made by considering where students are on the developmental continuum, how much progress they have made in relation to where they were at the time of the last assessment, and what is a reasonable expectation for them, taking into consideration their age and grade. A complex set of factors—that include child development understandings and knowledge of the literacy learning process—lead to the formulation of *reasonable expectations* for where students should be by what grade (see Figure 4–10).

Even within the context of traditional grading systems, however, standards-based reporting can be done. In my graduate teacher education courses, for example, I work within the framework of a traditional grading system. Figure 6–11 illustrates how I determine the grades for my students that I am required to report to the school. Each assignment (like the one in Figure 6–8, which has its own scoring guide to articulate the criteria and expectations) is allocated a set number of points. In this way, I use rubrics to guide the learning of my students for their individual assignments, I am able to inform my students of the overall course expectations, and I still fit within the system of which I am a part.

Conferences, Exhibitions, Museums

No written word can ever fully capture the power of a lived experience. Ways to demonstrate the richness of student learning beyond what written reports or grades can do are home-school conferences, student exhibitions, and "museum" presentations of student work.

Home-school conferences can be an avenue for helping parents and families understand what is involved in standards-based work. A home-school conference is a meeting between the teacher and the significant people in the student's life (including the student). It is a scheduled event to discuss the progress of the child as well as questions and concerns of family members. The child's work is on hand so that families have first hand contact with the concrete evidence of the child's learning. In the process of examining this work together, teachers, students, and

Standards-Based Report Card

Barbara Goldman
Principal

Nadine Kellogg
(1A) Assistant Principal

THE LILLIAN WEBER SCHOOL
P.S. 84 M

Reading Report to Parents
Third, Fourth, & Fifth Grade
1999-2000

Marking Period # _____

Student _____ Class _____
Teacher _____ Room _____

SCIENCE/SOCIAL STUDIES	Meets Standard	Approaches Standard	Area of Concern	Meets Standard	Approaches Standard	Area of Concern	Meets Standard	Approaches Standard	Area of Concern	Meets Standard	Approaches Standard	Area of Concern
Demonstrates observational skills by describing with details.												
Is able to record observations and conclusions.												
Participates in class discussions and group activities.												
Is building a knowledge of concepts.												
Teacher Comments												

NUMBER SYSTEM	Meets Standard	Approaches Standard	Area of Concern	Meets Standard	Approaches Standard	Area of Concern	Meets Standard	Approaches Standard	Area of Concern	Meets Standard	Approaches Standard	Area of Concern
Counts to _____.												
One-to-one correspondence to _____.												
Copies, understands, creates patterns.												
Notices patterns on a 100s chart.												
Solves story problems.												

ADDITION & SUBTRACTION STRATEGIES	Meets Standard	Approaches Standard	Area of Concern	Meets Standard	Approaches Standard	Area of Concern	Meets Standard	Approaches Standard	Area of Concern
Knows and uses combinations of ten.									
Knows and uses doubles.									
Can use a pattern to add ten to any number.									
Can use known facts as clues for subtraction facts.									
DATA	Meets Standard	Approaches Standard	Area of Concern	Meets Standard	Approaches Standard	Area of Concern	Meets Standard	Approaches Standard	Area of Concern
Can sort one or more objects by attribute.									
Can compare sets of data.									
Can make representations of data on paper.									
Can represent data with concrete materials.									
Can interpret information on a graph.									
KNOWLEDGE OF OTHER CONCEPTS STUDIED THIS PERIOD	Meets Standard	Approaches Standard	Area of Concern	Meets Standard	Approaches Standard	Area of Concern	Meets Standard	Approaches Standard	Area of Concern
Teacher Comments									

Figure 6–10

Grade Criteria for Seminar in Qualitative Research—Teacher Inquiry

Assignment	*Final Grade* Grades
Journal	18 points
Research review/analysis	20 points
Research question and references	15 points
Research design	40 points
Class participation/individual contribution	7 points

A+ = 98–100 points	B – = 80–82
A = 94–97	C+ = 77–79
A– = 90–93	C = 73–76
B+ = 87–89	C– = 70 – 72
B = 83–86	Unacceptable = below 70

Figure 6–11

their families can see and discuss how the work demonstrates progress in relation to standards as well as in relation to the student's own growth patterns.

Including students in home-school conferences by inviting them to present their work and to reflect on their growth is a particularly effective way for students to learn how to articulate what they know and can do. The more that they do this, the more they learn what standards of excellence look like; the more they come to understand and internalize what it means to produce high-quality work. They also learn how to articulate and reflect on what their *own* standards are—what they consider to be their best work, what areas they need to work on more, what is still "in progress," what plans should be formulated for next steps.

Home-school conferences focused on student work strengthen trust between home and school. They demonstrate to the student that there are no behind-the-scenes secrets; that nothing will be done "to" the student without frank, collaborative discussions concluding in mutual consent. They also help families understand the school's goals, purposes, and expectations while providing opportunities for families to share their perspectives, expectations, and dreams for their child's learning as well as their understandings of who their child is. This mutual sharing increases the trust needed for a sense of community to flourish in a school.

Other ways to communicate about what is involved in standards-based learning are through the group documentation of student learning that was described in Chapter 3 and through student exhibitions, or "museums," designed for students to display and explain their work. Many years ago, at the Bronx New School, my colleagues and I organized museums at the conclusion of individual classroom studies. Classrooms were temporarily transformed into museums containing exhibits of student-made books, experiments, artwork, constructions, puppet shows, videos, or musical performances that incorporated the learnings from a particular study. Students demonstrated what they learned at exhibitions as they displayed and explained their work to classmates, schoolmates, family members, and school faculty (Falk 1994).

I have now seen this way of working being carried out in many other classrooms in many schools that serve students from different backgrounds as well as ages—from the primary grades through high school. In each situation, the process of teachers, students, and their families looking at student work in relation to standards strengthens the capacities of the entire community to engage in and support powerful learning.

Chapter 7

Sitting Down to Score

Professional Learning Through Standards and Assessments

As standards-based reforms sweep the country and educators grapple with how to support an increasingly diverse student population to realize their academic and social potentials, there is a growing consensus among educators that professional development for teachers and administrators lies at the center of educational reform and instructional improvement. Over the last decades many reforms have focused on other aspects of schools and schooling: on providing guidance to schools about what students should be taught (content standards), on changing the structures and processes by which schools are held accountable (student performance standards, assessments, rewards, and penalties), or on creating new forms of governance structures that define and uphold accountability (site-based management, vouchers, charter schools). The assumption is that attention to these aspects of schooling will result in better student learning that will, in turn, be demonstrated by better student performance on tests.

What has been missing from such formulations, however, is attention to the actual teaching practices that produce better student learning. Recently this issue has received more attention because of an emerging body of research pointing to the quality of teaching as a critical influence on student performance. Numerous national studies report that increased professional knowledge on the part of teachers yields higher levels of student achievement (National Commission on Teaching and America's Future 1996, 1997). It is becoming increasingly clear that, far more than policies and organizational strategies—which only provide the backdrop in which educators are able to do their work—teachers' abilities to teach in powerful ways are essential to improved student learning.

This being the case, to ensure that all students have richer learning experiences and are enabled to reach more challenging goals, school systems are faced with an enormous task: developing teachers' capacities to teach so that a range of different learners are able to understand and effectively use new knowledge. Without investing in this kind of teacher learning, standards and standards-based assessment reforms—rather than raising achievement levels for all—could prove to have harmful effects in the long-term, particularly for those struggling students who are already least well served by the educational system.

What kind of professional learning opportunities develop the capacities of teachers to support more ambitious teaching and learning for all students? Over the years we have come to understand the limitations of the short-term teacher "training" model—the one-shot workshop or "expert" lecture—that transmits information and skills to passive recipients (Fosnot 1989; Giroux 1988; Lieberman 1995; Lieberman and McLaughlin 1992; Little 1992, 1993; Meier 1992). Increasingly, these forms of professional development are being replaced by a more long-range, capacity-building approach that offers "meaningful intellectual, social, and emotional engagement with ideas, with materials, and with colleagues both in and outside of teaching" (Little 1993, 10). In this approach, teachers get opportunities to focus on the application of general ideas, to try out new kinds of practices that bring them directly into contact with students and their work, and to collaboratively examine and reflect on their beliefs and their practices (Elmore 1996; Noble and Smith, 1994; Wilson 1990).

Working with performance assessment offers teachers exactly these kinds of opportunities for professional learning. In this chapter, I share studies and stories of how teachers' involvement with standards and performance-based assessment has enhanced their knowledge and their growth. I show how examining and assessing students' work—with other teachers, students, and sometimes their families—helps teachers understand what their students know and can do as well as how their students process learning. I describe how working with standards and standards-based assessments stimulates teachers to think about their curricular vision and to consider how different instructional approaches can be used to support the varying strengths, needs, and learning approaches of their students. And finally, I portray how teacher involvement in performance assessment supports reflection and provides opportunities for collaboration, which, in turn, enhances professionalism and strengthens abilities to engage in meaningful change.

Three different types of assessment initiatives that impact teacher learning are presented: teachers assessing student learning by observing, documenting, and collecting their work over time with classroom-based assessment frameworks; teachers scoring student responses to externally administered, standards-based performance tests; and teachers examining and validating their own practice by participating in the National Board of Professional Teaching Standards assessment and certification process.

Teacher Learning from Classroom-Based Assessment

For many years, teachers in classrooms across the country have been developing, using, and exploring the power of performance assessments. Processes for observing and recording children's behavior and for collecting and looking at children's work have been used—sometimes individually, sometimes in groups—to learn about children and their learning.

Classroom-based performance assessments are generally used in formative or summative ways: to inquire generally about the processes that go into learning—the learner's ideas, understandings, and approaches; or to evaluate the results of a specific learning experience. In either case, because they are embedded in the curriculum and because they call on students to apply knowledge and skills through real-life–like performances—such as essays, projects, or experiments—performance assessments provide a window into learners' thinking that can be useful to teachers' work.

Performance assessments help teachers learn how to identify and appreciate students' different strengths and approaches to learning. Some also provide teachers with a guide for their teaching—pointing out what strategies and behaviors to look for as students progress in their learning. Both types of performance assessments have been found to stimulate changes in the ways that teachers teach and provide occasions for colleagues to collaboratively reflect on and inquire about their own work.

A growing number of studies are documenting this relationship between teacher learning and classroom-based performance assessment (Allen 1998; Darling-Hammond, Ancess, and Falk 1995; Dorfman 1997; Falk 1994, 1998; Falk and Darling-Hammond 1993; Falk, MacMurdy, and Darling-Hammond 1995; Falk and Ort 1998, 1999; Kates 1999). Below I share some of the details that reveal the power and possibilities it offers.

Learning About the Strengths of Diverse Learners

When teachers get into the habit of collecting and reflecting on evidence about their students, they become more able to recognize and appreciate the different ways students learn. These understandings enhance teachers' abilities to provide effective instruction. An elementary dual language teacher explains:

Keeping observational records helps me to become aware that each child is learning at her own pace and that each child knows something and is good at something. I now gear my work more to each child, individualizing and giving children the support they need. (Falk, MacMurdy, and Darling-Hammond 1995, 35)

Teachers' appreciation for the strengths of different learners resulting from keeping track of student work also helps to safeguard against any bias that teachers may have about students' capabilities. Recognizing the varying strengths of diverse learners makes it harder to attach labels to children (Jose is a troublemaker) or to make all-inclusive judgments about them (Shanta can't read). These labels and judgments often have the unintended effect of becoming self-fulfilling prophecies—the child for whom adults have low expectations dutifully produces what is expected; the child who is labeled with a particular problem conforms to the image of her held by others. As a result, we inadvertently often set limits on the learning opportunities for these students. Although the intent may be to provide appropriate settings for students with special problems, the actual effect is to deny students access to challenging curriculum. This, in turn, constrains their abilities to develop as thinkers and limits their chances to achieve the rigorous expectations currently demanded by their school communities.

The story of Lara and her student Andre illustrates how observing and documenting student work in a systematic way helps to avoid turning concerns for students into perpetuating cycles of labels and limits. Lara, a kindergarten teacher in a New York City school, worried that four-year-old Andre was going to have problems with language development because he had a noticeable stutter. Her actual observations of Andre talking and listening in her class, however, demonstrated that Andre could communicate with his classmates and make himself understood. This evidence kept her from making unfounded judgments about his capabilities and helped to channel her concerns for Andre into support for his progress. She explains:

I knew he had difficulty with oral language and that emotionally he was tied up in knots. I worried he was going to have a hard time with language but I was wrong. Watching and documenting what he was doing showed me that he *didn't* have a hard time. The fact that I was really listening to him and writing down the things he was saying kept me from being biased about what he was capable of doing, from misjudging what he was actually doing, and from limiting learning opportunities for him based on my misjudgments. (Falk, MacMurdy, and Darling-Hammond 1995, 18)

In addition to safeguarding against bias, documentation of students and their work helps to understand students in the context of their culture and to appreciate students' strengths that might otherwise go unnoticed. This recognition subsequently leads to providing better supports for students' learning and to making more informed decisions that affect them and their futures.

This was the case for nine-year-old Kendall, a recent emigrant to New York City from Jamaica, who had low scores on standardized reading tests and was receiving extra supports through Title I assistance. Described by his classroom teacher as "nonfunctioning in literacy" and "unable to read, speak, or write," Kendall was referred for a special education evaluation.

However, Kendall's resource room teacher had a very different perspective of him and his oral language expression based on a broad array of evidence that she had collected. In addition to her documented observations of him and the samples of his work that she had saved, she also had notes from an interview that she had conducted with Kendall and his family. These proved to be critical in offering insights to his learning. Her records of the interview with Kendall's family presented information that revealed cultural differences between their home and the school, differences that were responsible for what Kendall's teachers saw as his "lack of spontaneity" in oral language. Kendall's family explained that their culture expected children to be quiet, polite, and obedient in school, to speak only when spoken to, and to do exactly what the teacher asked. When shared with the other teachers in the school, this description of Kendall's family's native country's expectations for appropriate school conduct caused the teachers to question whether Kendall's apparently lagging language development was the result of innate deficits in his abilities or the result of cultural differences.

The resource room teacher's own observations of Kendall gave strength to the cultural explanation of Kendall's behavior. Her documentation provided descriptions of him in diverse school contexts that revealed him expressing himself well in many situations and demonstrating considerable interest and ability:

> Kendall continues to be well behaved and very quiet in group situations. Yet he appears to be attentive and interested in all curriculum areas. When called upon, he will respond and read confidently. Otherwise, he will remain quiet and not contribute. He is beginning to initiate comments and questions in the classroom and small group situations. In the playground, however, he is verbal and socializes well. He is noticeably happier in one-to-one situations and when observing and listening. (Falk, MacMurdy, and Darling-Hammond 1995, 28)

This data filled in many of the gaps that were distorting the total picture of Kendall as a learner. It enabled those responsible for decisions about his future to see the strengths in him that had been missed by other conventional assessments, to see that he was making significant progress in his current class, and to avert an unnecessary referral to special education.

Providing a Guide for Teaching

Some classroom-based performance assessments provide a guide to essential aspects of learning simply by virtue of what they ask teachers to observe and record. *The Primary Language/Learning Record* (Barrs et al. 1988), *The Work Sampling System* (Meisels et al. 1993), and *The Early Literacy Profile* (New York State Education Department 1999)—to name just a few—are some of the assessments offering descriptions of critical strategies and behaviors that students utilize in their learning and that teachers need to look for as they interact with students. Evidence accumulated through these assessment frameworks can be used to inform instructional decisions. Because teachers are the primary assessors, the feedback about student learning is immediate and context-connected. There is no waiting for months, as after a test administration, to receive students' scores from the test publisher.

Teachers who work with such classroom-based performance assessments report them to have a powerful, positive impact on their teaching. Particularly welcomed are the types of assessments that provide age-appropriate expectations or signposts for the skills and strategies that students need. One primary grade teacher whose use of *The Early Literacy Profile* was studied in depth over the course of a year (Kates 1999, 20) explains, "An assessment like that gives you an indication of what you can teach toward. It gave me an idea of where the deficits, the holes, in my program are. If you don't have all of the criteria that you need to look for in front of you, then it's easy to leave something out." Other teachers who have worked with the same assessment also point to the explicit criteria of what to look for as being helpful in their instruction. A survey of sixty-six teachers who participated in a yearlong study of *The Early Literacy Profile* found that 98 percent of the teachers found the assessment to be a useful guide to their teaching (Falk and Ort 1999). Typical of their comments were:

> *The Early Literacy Profile* has been a guide for my teaching. It is the first real reading course I've ever taken. Through it I learned about all the strategies—semantic, syntactic, and phonetic cues—that go into reading.

> *The Early Literacy Profile* was useful to me in the sense that it helped me as a teacher to adjust my teaching techniques, to concentrate on some of the elements of literacy learning that I might have ignored, and to ask more penetrating questions to help the students. The scoring scales showed me specifics about where the students were as readers and writers.

Many teachers have found that classroom-based performance assessments offer much richer information for evaluations and decision making than the information provided through more conventional forms of assessments. Because classroom-based performance assessments include information about context and process as well as product, they present a fuller, more accurate, and fairer picture of student progress than conventional tests. A teacher explains:

> I learn much more about a child from the evidence I collect about his learning in the context of classroom activities than by the score received on the standardized test. With standardized tests there's no conferencing, no talking, no ongoing evidence of a student's learning. It's an isolated instance, a one-shot deal. You are basically looking at the product, no process. You don't get the picture of that whole child. You just get a score. But when I document what and how a student reads, when I examine her writing, and collect samples of projects or experiments, I get a broader range of understanding about what that child knows and can do. (Falk, MacMurdy, and Darling-Hammond 1995, 26)

Changing the Way Teachers Teach

The close-up look at students and their thinking offered through classroom-based performance assessment helps teachers change the way they teach. Many report that using performance assessments has heightened their awareness of both group and individual children's needs, thus enhancing their abilities to individualize instruction.

> Observing the strategies a child uses and those he doesn't helped me plan ways to help the child use those strategies he's not using now. I found myself planning with each student's needs in mind. (Falk, MacMurdy, and Darling-Hammond 1995, 15)

When assessments are embedded in meaningful, purposeful, and real-life experiences, teachers are freed from "teaching to the test" to support a broader vision of learning. They are able to expand the range of their instructional strategies and transform their classrooms to offer opportunities for students to engage in the kinds of behaviors that are more akin to how children learn. In studies of teachers who worked with both *The Primary Language Record* and *The Early Literacy Profile*, this was found to be the case. One teacher explains how using an observational assessment stimulated her to transform her classroom practices:

> Because the observation guidelines of the assessment asked me to observe kids while they were reading, I had to set up a structure in my classroom where kids had time to read independently and where they were engaged enough in the process that I could conference with them individually. (Falk, Ort 1999)

Another teacher notes how using *The Primary Language Record* pushed her to include more writing opportunities because the assessment called for regular observations in that area:

The assessment asked me to look at their writing. Before using it I never had opportunities for writing in my classroom. Now I make writing a big thing. (Falk, MacMurdy, and Darling-Hammond 1995, 38)

Teachers have noted other practices that they have instituted in their classrooms as a result of using curriculum-embedded assessments such as those mentioned above. Changes in literacy teaching practices include ensuring that each child has access to materials appropriate for their level of instruction rather than relying on whole class, one-size-fits-all instruction; using classroom libraries as a central aspect of the learning environment; providing regular opportunities for reading aloud; immersing classroom environments in print; using a range of media as vehicles for students' expression of their learning. Such teaching methods are a big departure from the heavy reliance on test practice booklets that so many of us have felt forced to use to prepare students for standardized tests.

Other changes in general teaching practices that have been ascribed to classroom-based assessment use include providing more opportunities for peer learning and collaboration; providing more choices for students in the learning environment; teaching in more integrated, interdisciplinary ways; and utilizing learning contexts that stretch beyond the walls of the school. The comments below explain how one teacher moved away from a teacher-centered classroom toward a learner-centered orientation as a result of using performance assessments in her classroom:

The way I teach and assess children is different from the way I taught and thought about it before. I started using an observational assessment framework because I was looking for some way to make my hunches about children more concrete. Before I had ideas about kids but no evidence. I felt like there must be a better way to do this. I found it through documenting children and their work. Based on what I see the child doing, and what the child and parents tell me, I now have information on what I can do to work together with them and to help the child. Sometimes it's as small a thing as knowing the kind of book a child likes to read so that I can suggest what to read next; or it's knowing that a child likes to reread so I know to be sure to do that with her. Having the evidence gives me more confidence in myself as a teacher because I have a real basis for my decisions. (Falk, MacMurdy, and Darling-Hammond 1995, 35)

Promoting Teacher Collaboration and Inquiry

Teachers using classroom-based performance assessments are as diverse a group in their thinking and experience as the children they are teaching. Nevertheless working with this type of assessment supports and challenges a variety of teachers to consider a host of questions and issues that tap into deeply rooted values influencing their teaching. This often leads them to engage in activities that foster professional inquiry. Some hold dialogue sessions within their schools at lunchtime, preparation periods, or after-school hours. Others participate in out-of-school activities—courses, study groups, and summer institutes—that feature group opportunities for exchanging ideas about teaching and assessment strategies.

A new sense of professional growth is often attributed to participation in these activities. This comment from one teacher attending a study group focused on assessment issues speaks to how such experiences foster the development of reflective practitioners:

> We read articles, talk about our reading, our work in the classroom, and about student work. As we discuss what we notice about children, we also begin to notice what we are noticing. We become more reflective about our own practice and more conscious about what we are learning. (Falk, MacMurdy, and Darling-Hammond 1995, 41)

The following story from a teacher study group demonstrates the power that reflection can have in shaping and reshaping teachers' beliefs, attitudes, and practices.

Denise, a teacher of eight- and nine-year-olds, raised a concern with her colleagues at a study group meeting about a group of boys in her class who read science books and talked together every day during the block of time devoted to the language arts. Although this was a time when the teacher encouraged children to read and write and talk together, she was particularly concerned about one boy in this group who still struggled with fluency in his reading. She was nervous that he was spending too much time talking and not enough time practicing his reading. In relating her concern to her colleagues, she realized that although she openly encouraged the stronger readers to converse, the very same process of chatting with others made her nervous if it was being done by weaker readers. She began to question whether it was fair to hold different standards of behavior for different kinds of students:

> Does that mean that a struggling reader shouldn't talk as much as a competent reader? I thought about the role of practice in learning to read and how I know that practice is very important. But I also thought about the role of choice in learning and how important it is for learner motivation. I thought about the relation between teacher choice and student choice. Classrooms generally are structured around teacher choice. I want to support and encourage student choice but if I decide this boy needs to practice his reading more, and all the while he wants to talk about books, I am taking away his right to make his own choice. And I never do this to competent readers. They get to choose what they want to do because their choices generally coincide with mine. (Falk, MacMurdy, and Darling-Hammond 1995, 42)

The implications of this tension are subtle but powerful; they have to do with issues of standards, autonomy, empowerment, and equity. Denise was torn between her responsibility to have all students achieve high standards and her equally strong commitment to provide all students with equitable learning opportunities. Having the opportunity to make choices—in this case, talking with others—is part of the children's right to learn; yet she was concerned that spending time talking would take away from the extra time and focus that weaker students need to be able to achieve high standards.

Denise eventually resolved this tension by structuring a time in her classroom when *all* students were required to engage in quiet, independent reading.

> I played around with ways to make that more appealing. And in fact, after a while, what I did worked! They all did settle into reading independently—to the extent that they were able. They all were willing to engage in doing what readers do—choose a book, sit and give it the attention it requires, trust that something is going to happen that is worthwhile. They all got over the hump of the resistance to reading—everybody would sit or lie on the floor and read. I looked up one day and said, "Wow, everybody's reading!" I know not everybody was reading the way a reading test would measure. But everybody was engaged with a book and this to me is an important measure of reading. (Falk, MacMurdy, and Darling-Hammond 1995, 42)

Denise is quick to point out that if she had not been looking at children in her classroom so closely and if she had not had the opportunity to discuss these issues in her study group, she most likely would not have noticed what these children were doing and would not have contemplated the important issues that were raised by the situation.

> What I came to realize when I was looking at this is that we put so much emphasis on reading and skills development in school we don't nurture other things that need to be nurtured in order for skills to develop. I really want to learn how to do this so that I can help all kinds of learners learn better. (Falk, MacMurdy, and Darling-Hammond 1995, 43)

Through Denise's systematic assessment of her students' learning and through discussions with her colleagues that helped to process this information, Denise came to powerful realizations that influenced her thinking and her practice. Is this not the goal of professional (indeed, any kind of) learning—to help individuals reach the point of questioning, searching, and seeking opportunities to reflect on and change what they do? Weaving performance assessment into the fabric of teaching helps teachers come to this juncture. Because they have experienced powerful learning themselves, they have a better sense of how to bring their students to this juncture as well. Documenting and reflecting on student work helps teachers better support student learning while, at the same time, it also supports teachers to engage in their *own* knowledge development. They experience firsthand what they come to understand is essential for all to learn well—that each requires a different look and a different pathway to growth.

Meeting the Challenge of Responsive Teaching: Teaching to the Child

Observing students in diverse contexts across the curriculum calls on teachers to take a closer look at themselves, their practices, their students, and students' learning. In doing so, the details of the learning process are revealed, clarifying the kinds of environments and practices that support different learners to learn in different ways. Rather than "teaching to the test," teachers are supported to "teach to the child."

Assessment processes that document students and their work provide a way for teachers to come to know their students well. They offer a window into children's thinking. They help us to see that children learn not by absorbing information that has been transmitted, but by making connections between new knowledge and the unique understandings and experiences of each individual. Performance assessments demonstrate that children are thinking, capable persons who are filled with impulse, interest, intention, wonder, curiosity, and creativity. They remind us that, if we are to support genuine learning, schools need to be thought of as more than mere institutions; they need to be places that offer opportunities to explore, question, experiment, search, problem pose, and problem solve in ways that connect to each individual.

Teacher Learning from Scoring Student Responses to Standards-Based Performance Tests

Involving teachers in scoring student responses to large-scale, standards-based performance tests offers rich opportunities to enhance teacher learning. Much of the teacher learning resulting from this activity takes place during the orientation process that precedes the actual scoring of student work. Scoring orientations are designed to teach potential scorers of standards-based performance tests how to use standards as a reference for evaluating students' responses. The goal of the orientation session is to ensure that scoring will be "reliable"—that everyone will develop common understandings of the criteria on which the scoring is based and that everyone will come to share common images of what each level of student performance looks like.

During scoring orientation, teachers, working in small groups, look over each assessment task to discuss the standards it assesses. They then review each task's criteria to discuss what students need to do to accomplish the task. Together, they examine sample student responses, referring to each task's rubric (or scoring guide) for descriptions of what the work looks like at different levels of proficiency. Discussing the work, detail by detail, they compare the evidence in each response to the rubric's indicators until they arrive at a consensus for a score. Inevitable differences in opinions and perspectives are mediated by the rubric's clearly articulated criteria for performance and the process' insistence that teachers always justify their evaluation using evidence from the student work. Although viewpoints may initially vary, after going through several sample responses teachers begin to consistently agree on the scores that they assign. Recurring consensus signals completion of the orientation. Only then do teachers move on to begin the actual independent scoring of tasks that is used to assign "official" exam scores.

In the course of scoring standards-based performance assessments, teachers learn to apply the same criteria and standards to the work of all their students. During this process, content standards, scoring rubrics, and student benchmark papers help teachers to think about their teaching and their students' learning. Content standards specify what the important aspects of a subject area are and provide broad conceptions of the discipline itself. Scoring rubrics make criteria explicit for distinguishing among different levels of performance in student work. The scoring activity itself requires looking for and seeing specific features of student work in terms of these criteria. Actual examples of student work at differing levels of performance provide benchmarks or reference points for how to establish to what degree standards are met. Learning how to use a rubric involves learning how to evaluate students' work based on evidence and relative to explicit standards, not based on unsubstantiated feelings or assumptions relative to other students' work.

Studies of teachers who have been involved in using standards and rubrics in scoring sessions such as these suggest that the process positively impacts teacher learning in a number of different ways (Falk and Ort 1998, 1999; Sheingold, Heller, and Storms 1997; Thomas et al. 1995). Participating in scoring helps teachers clarify goals and expectations for their teaching as well as for their students' learning, deepens their knowledge of their discipline, reveals important information about what their students know and can do, and offers overall insights that can be useful to their teaching. In addition, the highly professional atmosphere of scoring sessions strengthens teachers' sense of professionalism, heightens their understandings about the workings of the system of which they are a part, and reaffirms the central importance of teachers to the evaluation process. Instead of having to rely on outside "experts" to judge the outcomes of students' work, teacher involvement in scoring places assessment back into the domain of teaching, where it can be readily accessed to inform and support learning.

In 1996 I conducted a study with two hundred fifty teachers who participated in scoring sessions of the pilot administration of New York State's new statewide standards-based performance assessments. My colleagues and I obtained feedback from teachers who were part of these scoring sessions through observations during scoring, interviews with thirty participants, and an open-ended questionnaire administered to all who took part in the initiative (Falk and Ort 1998). Below are some of the findings that resulted from this study.

Clarifying Goals and Expectations for Teaching and Learning

One of the most valuable aspects of scoring standards-based performance assessments is the opportunity that scoring sessions provide for collegial conversations. The discussions that teachers have about standards, assessments, and student work in the context of scoring tests challenge them to learn about state or district expectations for their students and to clarify how their own views differ or agree. At the same time, these discussions present them with opportunities to consider how the standards' expectations might impact their teaching. Since state standards are, in a sense, political documents, reflecting a consensus opinion of diverse constituents, working with the standards challenges teachers to find a way to balance their individual views about what is important with the perspective of what is valued and valuable in their broader community. One middle school mathematics teacher expressed the views of many when she noted that:

> The discussion about the scoring rubrics was extremely useful. It was a great way of sharing ideas on what people think is important. (Falk and Ort 1998, 61)

Deepening Teachers' Knowledge of the Disciplines

Scoring student responses to assessment tasks also offers teachers a way to see how the big ideas embodied in standards actually play out in real student work. In addition, the experience helps them to develop shared understandings and a common language about the essentials of their disciplines.

The rubrics' frame for assessing student work guides teachers to use evidence, rather than personal feelings, as the basis for evaluations. One elementary teacher described how she transformed the way she evaluated student work as a result of participating in standards-based scoring:

> I moved away from thinking about work in an A, B, C, or D way, to thinking about the criteria for performance and the evidence that would justify my evaluation. (Falk and Ort 1998, 62)

Learning About Students and Their Work

Looking at student work in relation to standards helps teachers gain understandings about the strategies and approaches students bring to their learning. Of course, the ability to do this is contingent upon having worthy assessment tasks—tasks designed to be as contextualized as possible—asking students to show and explain their work, and allowing a wide range of students to be able to demonstrate their abilities. When the tasks possess these characteristics, the process of scoring student responses offers teachers a window into *what* their students know and can do as well as *how* their students actually do it.

Teachers who have been involved in scoring student work point to assessments that are "authentic" and performance-based as being most helpful for gaining insights into students' learning. Teachers surveyed in New York State overwhelmingly supported the areas of the new state tests that called for students to explain their thinking and to demonstrate their work. One middle school mathematics teacher said, "When students are expected to explain or support their answers, you begin to learn more about what they understand." A high school English teacher concurred and added, "I began to look more in-depth for what the students *could* do, rather than only focusing on what they *couldn't* do." The deeper look at young people's thinking offered through performance tasks helps teachers to gain a deeper respect for formerly unnoticed students' strengths and to appreciate the variety of ways students solve problems and express their ideas.

Teachers' visions of possibilities for "good work" also expand as a result of scoring. "Looking at student responses to the assessment tasks reinforced the idea that good work can look very different and can take on many forms," noted an elementary teacher who administered and scored a math, science, and technology task. Teachers' perspectives on expectations for student performance are also broadened because they look at student work from different locales and from a variety of racial, socioeconomic, and linguistic backgrounds. "I learned so much from seeing the work of students other than my own," said one high school English teacher. Another of her colleagues added, "The most valuable part of the scoring session was learning about the differences and similarities of the populations of different school districts." (Falk and Ort 1998, 62)

Other benefits of scoring noted by teachers are attributed to the nature of the assessment tasks used. Some teachers point to the clear and public articulation of expectations in tasks as helping them to help students achieve:

> When the expectations are very clear, it seems students will meet them. I learned that all students can achieve. (Falk and Ort 1998, 62)

Other teachers point to tasks that offer students multiple ways to demonstrate their knowledge, skills, and understandings about many dimensions and kinds of learning as being most informative and useful. Because these kinds of tests provide opportunities for a wide range of students to reach toward higher standards, they also allow a wide range of students to actually demonstrate higher standards. "I learned that low-achieving students can experience success as well as express an element of critical thought that I never believed possible," reported one high school English teacher.

With well-designed standards-based performance assessments, a broad range of students are offered a variety of ways to demonstrate their proficiencies. Some teachers consider this to be an essential element of a fair test. "I have changed my attitude," said an elementary teacher who participated in a statewide scoring session. "This is a fairer way of assessing." Discussions of fairness also lead to consideration of even broader equity issues. If all students need to prepare for these more challenging exams, then all students need to have equal opportunities to experience more challenging learning. An elementary teacher raised this issue in her comments:

> This assessment allows many entry points for kids who are at all levels. Hopefully, this will encourage middle and high schools to begin detracking and allowing all children access to the same curriculum and standards. (Falk and Ort 1998, 62)

Developing Insights to Support Teaching

The process of scoring students' work strengthens teachers' understandings of what students should know and be able to do in ways that help teachers to develop more cohesive programs of instruction. Some teachers attribute this to the conversations during and before scoring. As one teacher remarked:

> The discussions that took place during the scoring session made me more aware of expectations for good teaching and learning. They were a catalyst for my planning and for better teaching. (Falk and Ort 1998, 62)

Many teachers say that participation in scoring motivates them to focus on needed changes in their practice. One teacher's comments reflect this view:

> I think I'm going to be teaching a little differently now: group work activities; making sure students understand the concepts of what they're doing; not looking just for the wrong or right answer. That's very important and so is how students are arriving at their answer. (Falk and Ort 1998, 62)

Other teachers credit the process of looking at student work in relation to standards as helping them become more aware of aspects of their discipline and practice that they feel are in need of strengthening. "Scoring student work for this exam has encouraged me to take a closer look at the way I teach math," said an elementary teacher. A middle school mathematics teacher concluded, "I need to focus instruction more on problem solving." And some teachers find support for what they are already doing. Said an elementary grade teacher, "It confirms and supports the way I teach and makes me realize that I need to keep asking kids for details—getting them to find the specific evidence from their reading."

The benefits of standards-based performance assessments that teachers experience while scoring student work often inspire them to institute changes in their own classroom-based assessment practices. They do this not just to better prepare their students for tests but to improve the teaching and learning that goes on in their classrooms. "I plan to give kids rubrics detailing what makes 'quality' work," said one elementary teacher. "I will provide more opportunities for revision, self-analysis, and evaluation," said another. A middle school teacher vowed "to make the open-ended questions I ask clear enough to get the information I want to get from the students. I will also make grading criteria very clear, very related to the question, and available to students ahead of time." A high school mathematics teacher who recognized the value of student explanations said, "I will do more testing requiring justifications—help students to become more comfortable explaining their understandings."

Strengthening Teachers' Sense of Professionalism

Teachers' discussions about students' work in relation to standards in contexts such as scoring conferences offer them opportunities to collaborate, to learn from each other, and to validate their knowledge as competent professionals. The comments of those who took part in the scoring sessions for state tests that I studied demonstrate teachers' appreciation of this: "Meeting with dedicated, concerned teachers was most valuable to me," noted one high school teacher. "I learned from their positive attitudes, from discussing concerns about my students and about future directions for my discipline."

Looking together at student work in relation to standards also provides teachers with time and a way to learn about new practices and educational processes. "I don't think you can underestimate the need that folks have for getting together and having quality time to reflect on all of the changes that are happening in our schools," said one high school social studies teacher. The discussions, debates, and sharing of ideas about what is important and how it is demonstrated that take place during scoring processes provide a structure for teachers to engage in the dialogue and inquiry that are recognized essentials of professional growth. As one high school teacher reported:

Scoring sessions provide valuable professional dialogue. It is a great way to do teacher inservice. (Falk and Ort 1998, 63)

Facilitating Change

Group processes for assessing student work can galvanize teachers' support for change by showcasing proposed directions for change in teaching and assessment in ways that directly connect to students and their work. When the standards are well developed and the assessments are performance-based, scoring student work gets at the core of what teaching and learning is about. Such involvement heightens the probability that teachers—who are, after all, the ones who must ultimately enact any change—will come to understand and embrace the change (Cohen, Stern, and Balaban 1997; Elmore 1996). Lauren Resnick emphasizes this fact in her writings about teachers' work with standards:

> Standards documents, even elegant ones with benchmarks and commentary, can affect achievement only if the standards come to be held as personal goals by teachers and students. . . . That will happen only if a concerted effort is made to engage teachers and students in a massive and continuing conversation about what students should learn, what kinds of work they should do, and how well they should be expected to do it. (Resnick 1995, 113)

Involving teachers in scoring assessments thus sends an important message to teachers. It signals that teachers can be active participants in shaping the direction of school change. It acknowledges the critical role teachers play in education reform. It puts teachers in their rightful place: at center stage in the school improvement process.

Using Standards-Based Performance Assessment to Reflect on and Strengthen Teachers' Work

As the use of standards and performance-based assessments for students has spread, a parallel development has been taking place for teachers. Through the National Board for Professional Teaching Standards certification process, a process that recognizes accomplished teaching, teachers are offered opportunities to reflect on and learn about their practice. National Board for Professional Teaching Standards certification is a process of documenting teaching practice in relation to rigorous standards that reflect excellence in teaching. It involves developing a professional portfolio and taking a written examination that demonstrates how teachers use standards in their everyday work. The portfolio and the examination are evaluated by peers knowledgeable about how to assess work in relation to standards.

Standards Developed by Teachers to Represent the Best of Teaching

The portfolio and the examination consist of a set of tasks designed to embody the National Board standards for one of thirty certification areas that are structured around student developmental levels and subjects taught. Developed by a committee of teachers, teacher educators, developmental experts, and leaders in the disciplinary fields, the standards represent consensus about an overall vision of excellence in teaching as well as consensus in each certification field about the critical aspects of teaching that distinguish the practice of accomplished teachers. In contrast to the endless lists of facts or esoterica often found in other standards documents, these standards speak to the essentials of great teaching—what a teacher should know and be able to do—in ways that resonate profoundly with those who are closest to classroom practice. My colleague Lorraine Scorsone, one of the first teachers in the early 1990s to become National Board certified, explains:

> When I read [the standards] I literally got goose bumps! I felt so proud to be a teacher! For the first time in my life I read a document that described the moment-by-moment life of a teacher. It described everything from the littlest nuance to the larger philosophic underpinnings of teaching. For me, [the standards] were tremendously validating because in [them] I saw all my years of study and schooling put in practice. It was as if the collective wisdom of all teachers were articulated and demystified for all interested people.

Tasks That Call on Teachers to Synthesize, Apply, and Demonstrate Knowledge

In much the same way that high-quality, standards-based performance assessments call on students to demonstrate in real-life situations what they know and can do, the National Board portfolio and examination tasks ask teachers to show what they do to support students' learning in the daily context of their classroom. Developing the portfolio entails a good deal of reflection on teaching practices as well as a close look at students' work. Through written narratives, videotapes, and analyses of children's work, candidates are called upon to think about, demonstrate, and reflect on their knowledge of children, child development, subject matters, and teaching. They also show how they use assessment to inform their teaching, how they respond to the varying needs of the different students in their class, and how they establish family, community, and professional partnerships. Figure 7–1 is a listing of the portfolio and examination entries required for the Early Childhood/Generalist certificate.

NBPTS Certificate Overview

EARLY CHILDHOOD GENERALIST

The **Early Childhood/Generalist (EC/Generalist)** certificate is designed for teachers of students ages 3–8. The National Board Certification process is voluntary and is open to public and private school teachers from pre-kindergarten through grade 12.

Status of This Certificate
The National Board has developed standards for what accomplished Early Childhood/Generalist teachers should know and be able to do. The National Board will be offering the EC/Generalist certificate during the 1998–99 school year. The EC/Generalist portfolio is available to teachers as of June 1, 1998. Teachers wishing to apply for National Board Certification in this certificate field during the 1998–99 school year must submit a completed application by December 1, 1998. All portfolio materials must be submitted to NBPTS by April 16, 1998. The assessment center portion of the assessment will be administered during the summer of 1999.

The Assessment Process
The assessment is performance-based and designed to evaluate the complex knowledge and skills of teaching described in the NBPTS standards. The assessment process consists of two components: the portfolio and the one-day assessment center. The certification decision will be based on candidate performance as judged against the NBPTS standards for accomplished practice.

The Portfolio
The portfolio of the Early Childhood/Generalist assessment gives teachers the opportunity to present a sample of their actual classroom practice over a specified time period. The portfolio consists of six entries:

- **Introduction to Your Classroom Community**—Teachers are asked to show how they structure their time, establish rules and routines, and organize space and materials in ways that promote children's social development, mutual respect, and emerging independence. Teachers submit a written commentary and an accompanying videotape that highlights their interaction with children.
- **Reflecting on a Teaching and Learning Sequence**—Teachers submit a written commentary and supporting artifacts that show how they nurture children's growth and learning as they explore an extended theme or topic drawn from at least two content areas—Social Studies and the arts.
- **Engaging Children in Science Learning**—Teachers are asked to feature a learning experience that engages children in the investigation of a science concept. Central to teachers' written responses is a detailed examination of a learning experience they

Figure 7–1. National Board of Professional Teaching Standards Early Chhildhood/Generalist certificate portfolio requirements

videotape. They are also asked to describe how this learning experience is embedded within an ongoing series of activities designed to promote children's understanding of science concepts and processes. Teachers submit a videotape and written commentary.

- **Examining a Child's Literacy Development**—Teachers are asked to present the ways in which they foster literacy development in their classroom. They are also asked to analyze selected work samples from one child and discuss the steps they would take to support the featured child's literacy development. Teachers submit a written commentary and the work samples from the selected child.
- **Documented Accomplishments Exercise I**—Teachers submit descriptions and documentation of those activities and accomplishments that illustrate their commitment of their students' families and the communities of their students. In addition, teachers are asked to compose two brief interpretive summaries related to these accomplishments.
- **Documented Accomplishments Exercise II**—Teachers submit descriptions and documentation of those activities and accomplishments that illustrate their commitment to the teaching profession. In addition, teachers are asked to compose two brief interpretive summaries related to these accomplishments.

The Assessment Center

The EC/Generalist assessment center exercises examine content knowledge and pedagogical content knowledge specified in the NBPTS standards. There are four written exercises:

- **Observing Children**—Teachers will observe a videotape of preschool children playing in their classroom. The prompts will tap the teachers' capacities to observe children and draw inferences about their development.
- **Constructing Curriculum**—Using the context of their own classroom, teachers will be asked to develop math curriculum using a specified concept. This exercise will tap teachers' capacities to use their knowledge of the children in their class, math content, and educational resources to develop curriculum.
- **Using Assessment Information**—Teachers will analyze case information describing a seven-year-old second-grade child. The exercise will tap teachers' capacities to evaluate and synthesize assessment information from multiple sources, pose questions, and identify strategies for collecting additional information.
- **Analyzing Children's Work Samples**—Teachers will analyze work samples from a kindergarten child. The work samples will include drawings, child dictations explaining the drawings, and a transcript of a conversation with the teacher. The samples will reveal the development of a child's understanding of a particular science concept. The teachers' responses will display their ability to analyze a child's learning in the area of science.
- Teachers are given 90 minutes to complete each of the exercises.
- Four scores are reported, one for each exercise.

National Board for Professional Teaching Standards   July 1998

Figure 7–1.   (Continued)

Tasks Model Features of Good Teaching

By asking candidates to demonstrate their knowledge and skills in real-life experiences, the National Board assessment tasks distinguish themselves as a learning challenge. However, a close look at the design of the portfolio entries reveals other qualities that are responsible for making this assessment such a powerful learning experience. The portfolio is notable for its clarity of explanation, its elaboration of details, and its advance notice of requirements for success. Each task is introduced with an explanation of the purposes for the task and the standards the task is designed to assess. A detailed description of the nature of the task and of what the candidate needs to do to complete it are provided. Criteria and guiding questions for each part of the task are presented. Recommendations for how to proceed through the task are offered, and a description of how the response will be scored is included.

The National Board tasks are opportunities for teachers to demonstrate their competencies in multiple ways. Application of knowledge, evaluation, analysis, and reflection are both called for as well as promoted by the very nature of the tasks. Teachers who go through the certification process must take a hard look at their teaching practices and become very specific about describing as well as documenting them. Evidence is required to back up all that the candidate has to say. Every step of the process is purposeful and carefully crafted to stimulate reflection, to go deeper into developing and then demonstrating understandings of what is entailed in teaching and learning. No facts can be memorized, no "right answers" produced, to achieve a passing score that entitles one to National Board certification. No "perfect" portfolio is required. Only thoughtful reflection on how the standards for accomplished teaching are either present, or not present, in carefully documented work of both the teacher and her students can demonstrate that a teacher has the knowledge, skills, and reflectiveness to identify her practice as meeting the standards.

Offering Insights into Teaching Practice

Some years ago I attended a conference where I heard one of the National Board's pioneer candidates make a presentation. She told the audience that "outside of the birth of my children, this has been the most powerful learning experience of my life." Other teachers who have gone through the process have similar things to say. A survey of sixteen New York City teachers who went through the National Board certification process in 1999 found that *all* of them thought their experience enhanced their professional development. Some noted that "the experience forced me to think more deeply about my practice" and "caused me to focus and be more aware of the standards that make for 'good teaching.'" Others pointed to how going through the process caused them to gain deeper insights about teaching: "This process has thrust me into the role of an inquisitive observer, wanting to learn what is understood by the student." Almost every candidate expressed a desire to continue the process for another year if they did not achieve a passing score the first time. They attributed their commitment to the value of the process itself: of the changes in their teaching as they conscientiously tried to ensure the incorporation of the standards in their practice; of the systematic reflection that has now become an automatic habit of mind; of the increased learning they're observing in their classrooms (Falk, Mann, and Scorsone in press).

A New Form of Professional Accountability

Because it systematically documents the best of what we do every day and who we are as educators, the National Board certification process is not only authentic but meaningful. The high expectations of the standards serve as a signpost that can be used to hold ourselves accountable. They make the elements of quality teaching explicit, bringing them out of the private realm of individual teachers' artistry or intuition and instead making them part of a conversation that can deepen our collective understandings about quality teaching, validate our expertise, and improve both our and our students' learning. The standards and the assessment process around them help to define, empower, and improve our profession. As my colleague Lorraine has said, "I believe holding ourselves accountable and having high expectations can only improve our field and how we're viewed. Sometimes politicians, the press, and the general public at large seem to police schools without adequate knowledge of the complexities of our profession. Too often we are told what and how to teach by people who have never set foot in the classroom. The standards not only give voice to excellence, they allow teachers to determine and define and inform exemplary teaching."

Empowering Teachers Through Professional Community

Participating in the work that has grown up around National Board standards and assessments not only gives voice to teachers but helps to break down the isolation that has been a trademark of our profession. National Board work offers teachers a chance to become part of a broader educational community. In standards development work, in mentoring groups that have sprung up around the country to support candidates' journey through the certification process, and in the portfolio and examination scoring sessions conducted almost entirely by teachers, teachers are able to share ideas and have collegial exchanges. These experiences offer opportunities to access a larger professional vision that stimulates growth. The comments of one Boston teacher who just completed a scoring session of portfolio items seems to express these sentiments well: "I'm absolutely exhausted—but can't wait to get back to my classroom. I just wish the other teachers in my building could have had the same experience: imagine how powerful that would be" (Kelley 1998, 2).

Professional Learning *Is* the Job

In "Professional Development *Is* the Job," Anthony Alvarado enumerates ways that educators can create change in order to support students' learning. Children's abilities to learn depend in large part on teachers' abilities to teach. "We will have to find ways of getting deeply into the specifics of how to help students master subject matter . . . and we will have to create contexts that support changes in thinking and pedagogy on the part of teachers" (Alvarado 1998, 18).

A focus on how to better support teacher learning is critical to efforts aimed at improving student learning. Schools' abilities to develop students depend on the existence of teachers who are knowledgeable about the critical elements of learning and who can employ the strategies that are needed to connect these elements with the understandings of diverse learners. Standards-based and performance-based assessments help teachers to develop this knowledge and these skills. By clarifying goals and purposes, by making expectations explicit, by requiring knowledge to be applied in real-life contexts, and by providing many different ways to demonstrate abilities and skills, standards-based and performance-based assessments lay the groundwork for better teaching. While they do not ensure that teachers will make the necessary connections with the understandings of their students that result in genuine learning, they certainly point teaching in that direction.

Standards-based and performance-based assessments, in their variety of contexts and formats, support teacher learning in several ways. By virtue of what they ask teachers to assess about their students or about themselves, they provide a guide to essential aspects of the learning process. In addition, this kind of assessment leads teachers to engage in evidence-based work—to collect and rely on authentic student or teacher work to reflect on and inform their instructional decisions. By asking teachers to examine their own practice or the work of their students in relation to standards, teachers increase their knowledge of individual students, become better informed about their students' capacities, and receive guidance about what they need to do next to support students' forward development.

I predict that continued use of high-quality standards and performance assessments over time will help teachers become better informed about teaching and learning. As we become more expert about teaching, due in part to what we learn from using standards-based and performance-based assessments, we can expect to witness continued improvement and progress on the part of students. Not only will our overall pedagogical capacity be enhanced, but control of assessment will be brought back into our hands, away from the "outside experts" and commercial testing companies that presently dominate the assessment process.

Well-developed standards-based and performance-based assessments initiate a dynamic process—an "upward-spiraling double helix" of standards and performance that has the potential to transform the culture of teaching (Kelly 1998, 3). As this transformation takes place across the continuum of teaching—from preservice teacher preparation programs through the careers of experienced

Sitting Down to Score Standards-Based Performance Assessments

- Deepens teachers' understandings of:

  standards
  their discipline
  their students
  their teaching

- Strengthens teachers' sense of professionalism:

  fosters collegial dialogue centered on teaching and learning
  validates professional knowledge
  sets up a structure to keep inquiry alive

- Facilitates lasting change:

  puts teachers at the center of the change process
  provides a forum to facilitate meaningful engagement with new ideas
  offers time and a process for taking ownership of new ideas
  builds capacity for new practices rather than simply mandating changes
  gets to the heart of the matter—teaching and learning

- Uses resources efficiently:

  teacher involvement in standards-based performance assessment equals
  professional learning

Figure 7–2

teachers—a new vision of teaching will take root in the hearts and minds of teachers by the millions. This vision will be about a seamless connection between assessment, context, teaching, and learning. Through the linkage of evaluation and practice, teachers and students will develop the capacity to monitor and take responsibility for their own learning. If the expectations are appropriate, the evaluations are fair, and the environment is maintained to be risk-free, then teachers and children will feel comfortable and confident. Success will be demystified, attainable, and doable through a variety of pathways. Effort will be the primary requirement. This is what genuine accountability should be about—a learning experience for all who are involved.

Chapter 8

Getting to the Heart of the Matter

Challenges for Educators in Challenging Times

Indeed we live in challenging times. In the face of increased public scrutiny, expanded demands, and unparalleled consequences for what we and our students are expected to do, many educators are confused or angry or scared or demoralized about how to proceed with our work. How do we handle the pressures of expectations that our students meet greater challenges than ever before? How do we secure adequate resources for our increasingly diverse student population to meet those expectations? How do we resist efforts to standardize in order to preserve the art of teaching and the complexities of powerful learning? How do we maintain balance between individual and community needs? How do we draw on the positives of standards-based initiatives and minimize the harmful practices that increasingly accompany them?

Chapters of this book have shared stories and information about how standards and assessments, when developed, used, and supported appropriately, can benefit student learning and teacher growth. Other chapters of this book have also shown how standards and their related assessments, when not used wisely, have the potential to inflict great harm. The dilemma of this duality is expressed well by the Chinese ideograph for the word *change*. Within the word are two symbols: one for opportunity, the other for danger. The use and misuse of standards and assessments presents an apt case in point.

In this final chapter, I review some of the dilemmas and challenges presented to us by standards-based work. It is my belief that if we embrace these challenges, we can help to shape the direction of the standards movement toward genuine educational improvement.

Challenge #1: Defining Standards to Incorporate Principles of Learning and Issues of Social Justice

The first challenge is to clarify and advocate for a definition of "standards," one that embodies principles of learning and that takes into account issues of social justice. Currently the term means different things to different people. To some, *high standards* simply means teaching more and harder content through the same methods that have been used in the past—recalling facts, drilling on skills, answering other people's questions. To others, *high standards* also implies more and higher gates to success.

Yet there are many who disagree with these definitions and who also disagree with how standards-based initiatives are being used. Many of those who disagree actively oppose standards and standards-based work. Others simply refrain from dealing with standards and standards-based work at all. I suggest here another approach: to embrace the positives of standards-based work while also rejecting the harmful aspects; to engage in the conversation and work about standards so that we can have an impact on defining the meaning and shaping the direction that these new initiatives take. I suggest that we bring to the standards conversation the goals and purposes that *we* hold dear.

In the early part of this century, Jean Piaget described the purpose of education as:

> the creation of men and women who are capable of doing new things, not simply repeating what others have done—men and women who are creative, inventive and discoverers . . . who can be critical, can verify, and not accept everything they are offered. (in Greene 1978, 80)

High standards to many of us means just this—learning that leads to deep understandings about the world, enables students to problem solve and problem pose about issues and questions that are purposeful and of significance, and leads to the "having of wonderful ideas" (Duckworth 1987). High standards also means goals that are developmentally appropriate, informed by knowledge of how children learn, developed broadly to focus on essentials rather than on countless items of information students are expected to memorize. Concretely, this translates into teaching practices that connect skill development to purposeful learning and that provide many pathways to knowledge for diverse learners. High standards, in the words of Paolo Friere, means learning about the *world* as well as the *word* (Freire 1973).

When these purposes and definitions guide standards' development and use, standards and related assessments can be of great benefit to teaching and learning. They can be an opportunity to learn about students and how they learn. They can be a vehicle for educational communities to clarify and develop shared meanings about goals, purposes, and expectations. They can be a catalyst for professional learning and a means to school renewal.

Challenge #2: Teaching the Way That Children Learn

To help students achieve high standards defined in this way, another challenge we face is to focus attention on the quality of the teaching and learning process. Old methods cannot be relied on now to attain new and more challenging goals. We need to break away from conceptions of learning that constrain teaching to little more than test preparation. Granted, students need to acquire much of the knowledge and to master many of the skills that are asked for in current tests. But the route to this goal is much more complex than simply working through test-preparation programs.

If powerful learning is to occur, students need much broader and deeper experiences than test preparation can provide. They need to experience rich contexts for learning that value their questions, their wonderings, their noticings, their inventions. They also need to be offered multiple pathways and entry points to learning that are appropriate to their different strengths and styles of learning, their different cultural and linguistic backgrounds.

Contexts that enable this kind of learning are rich with materials, social relations, and experiences of the real world. They utilize the resources and "funds of knowledge" of children's families and communities. They release the impulse to learn in the learner and help connect the learner to the world and to ideas. Patricia Carini has called this kind of teaching "teaching to let learn." It is teaching that builds on what the learner *cares* about and that supports and extends that caring (Carini 1987).

This kind of learning requires time—time for students to make connections within the idiosyncrasies of their own thoughts; time to actively discover relatedness among events; time for the expressing, questioning, likening, remembering, appreciating, enjoying, discerning, and imagining that leads to the development of deep understanding.

Time is also needed to enable learners to make mistakes. Mistakes, in the context of learning, are opportunities—a point highlighted by a recent conversation with my colleague Hubert Dyasi, director of the City College Workshop Center for Inquiry Education. He told me the story of the scientist who invented the cure for syphilis. It took that scientist more than eight hundred tries before he came up with the cure. After several hundred tries, the scientist was able to kill the syphilis virus but, alas, also killed the rat who was its host. So the scientist kept on, he persevered, each time changing the variables just a bit. It took another several hundred tries before he eventually found the cure.

Time is essential for powerful learning. We need time in our learning lives to create new ideas, to understand and eventually come to own what we learn.

Challenge #3: Assessing to Inform and Support Learning

The teaching challenge cannot be fully met without addressing another challenge—the assessment challenge. This challenge needs to be met because assessment is an integral part of good teaching—teachers must know learners well to effectively make connections between what they previously understood and what they are trying to learn.

Good assessment reveals what students know and can do, the strategies they use, and the understandings they bring to their learning. Good assessment helps teachers bridge knowledge of the learner with important content knowledge and skills. Earlier chapters of this book have discussed the limitations of traditional tests—how limited they are in regard to what they reveal and how they call attention away from the wholeness and activeness of learners' efforts to make sense of the world. We have seen how tests' definitions of knowledge and skills strongly influence what is taught in schools and what students are expected to learn. We have seen how in many places "It is accepted without question that neither teaching nor subject matters nor education have any purpose or meaning beyond what tests measure" (Carini 1987, 9).

This brings to mind a fourth-grade classroom that I visited recently. As I entered it, I noticed, on a table by the door, a stack of practice tests for the upcoming district and state exams. Despite the fact that this event was fast approaching, the teacher of this class had the courage to not allow it to interfere with the children's learning. The children were in the midst of doing independent research projects. When I walked into the room, Elena, one of the students, approached me. She was doing a study on homeless people and having a difficult time obtaining information. In response to her request for help I suggested that she find out what organizations serve the homeless and then call them to get information. As I accompanied her to the school office to use the phone, I discovered that she did not know what a telephone book is or how to use one. I then showed her how it is organized into different sections and how the words are listed alphabetically.

While we were working, I thought of those stacks of worksheets on the table by the door in her classroom. Searching through the telephone book, contacting organizations, seeking, processing, and sharing information offered this little girl a much more interesting and meaningful way to practice the skills she needs for her state test than most of the activities on those practice sheets. How narrow, and in many ways ludicrous, it is that schools focus so much attention, time, and resources on testing and on test preparation when comparatively so little emphasis, guidance, and support is given to nurturing the learning that is so abundant in real life.

Within this story are important assessment challenges for us all—most importantly, to keep external testing from driving our teaching away from what we know is real learning. But this is not the only challenge we must address. We also need to develop new assessments that have the capacity to capture the richness and fullness of meaningful learning and the abilities of those who express their understandings in different ways. We need these kinds of assessments for the work in our classrooms as well as for accountability purposes.

Earlier chapters of this book have discussed how difficult this task proves to be, especially in regard to assessments intended for reporting our progress to the public. Regardless of the difficulty, however, we must persist until we are able to create assessments that validly demonstrate what students know and can do in ways that inform and support teaching. We must persist until we have assessments and *systems* of assessment that rely predominantly on asking students to demonstrate their knowledge in ways that are closer to those used in real life—to solve problems, explain ideas, and apply understandings and skills. We must persist until we have assessments that are learning experiences for students as well as their teachers. We must persist until we have assessments that evaluate student progress by considering multiple forms of evidence and that are flexible enough to allow different students and schools to demonstrate their knowledge in multiple ways.

But even the best assessments can be harmful if they are not used wisely and well. This points leads to another challenge.

Challenge #4: Lessening the High Stakes Attached to Assessments

Assessment data should be used primarily to inform teaching decisions, to marshal resources for students in need, and to evaluate school practices. Current policies that rely solely on assessment results to determine high-stakes consequences for students—decisions about tracking, grade promotion, graduation, or referrals to special education—or for educators—financial rewards or job security—will end up doing more harm than good.

Throughout this book I have cited numerous studies and reports that caution us against coupling high stakes with standards and assessments because this practice increases student failure and dropout rates. I have referred to many studies that demonstrate the damaging effects of retention policies. I have discussed theories of learning and motivation that point to the harm that punishments and rewards inflict on genuine motivation for learning.

Students who are poor are hardest hit by these practices because disproportionate numbers of them are low scorers on tests. But their problems of low performance on tests cannot be remedied with these punitive solutions.

Many factors influence learning and performance, many of which are common to students who are poor. Poor students often live in communities that do not have adequate housing, health care, or employment. Their families frequently do not have access to the kinds of resources, experiences, and opportunities that prepare children to do well in school. When they enter the school doors they are further disadvantaged: Poor children are, as a group, the most likely to attend schools that have substandard facilities, inadequate materials, outdated texts, overcrowded classrooms, and that are under-funded. (In Texas, for example, the hundred wealthiest school districts spend about $4,200 more per student than the hundred poorest school districts [Chase 2000, 44]). To make matters worse, statistics show that schools attended by poor children are staffed by disproportionately high percentages of underqualified, uncertified teachers (National Commission on Teaching and America's Future 1996). Thus, children of the poor, those most in need, receive the least resources and supports to assist them in their learning.

Given these conditions, it is no surprise that poor children are disproportionately represented among low test scorers on most national and other large-scale tests. New standards-based assessments that more clearly reveal the nature of students' skills and understandings than traditional tests do are likely to expose, even more starkly, the learning inadequacies that poor children suffer because of the enormous burdens and challenges they face simply because they are poor.

But should we not test poor children because we already know that they most probably will not do well? No. Rather, I suggest that we place our emphases on remedying what we already know to be true. I suggest that we focus our educational as well as societal efforts on infusing massive supports to enhance learning and all aspects of living for those poor students who need it the most. Meanwhile, in regard to tests, I suggest that we not attach such high stakes to their outcomes. Given the fact that there are so many factors that contribute to why poor students, as a group, tend to be low scorers on tests, and given the fact that these factors extend far beyond the influence of students' efforts and even the efforts of their schools, we should not punish the students. We should not use poor children, many of whom are from minority backgrounds, "as cannon fodder in the education accountability wars" (Chase 2000, 44).

But that is exactly what tests with high stakes consequences do. Regardless of how admirable it may seem to raise expectations for all students, how reasonable is it to expect students and their teachers to meet more rigorous standards in only a few short years? How can they be expected to compensate for all the burdens of poverty that have contributed to the inadequacies of their entire past school careers? Do we realize that immediate tough consequences attached to tests such as grade retention or failure to graduate jeopardize the futures of huge percentages of students, that the consequences of not graduating high school for many students may be minimum wage jobs, welfare, or jail?

To be opposed to high-stakes tests is not to be opposed to assessment or accountability. Rather it affirms the need to have accountability mechanisms that are fair. Fair accountability acknowledges the social inequalities in our cities and nation. Fair accountability uncouples high stakes from standards and assessment use. Fair accountability uses standards and assessments to give us information that can improve student learning. It relies on standards and assessments as only one element of a broad range of information used to make decisions about students' futures and to allocate supports for students and schools.

Challenge #5: Advocating for Equitable Opportunities to Learn

We cannot help students reach more challenging goals without providing more resources to support their learning. It is cruel and unfair to demand more rigorous standards for students without at the same time providing them with the resources they need to accomplish these goals. This means ensuring that *all* students have access to schools with adequate funding, smaller classes, updated books, technology, and other learning materials; to school environments that are caring and safe; and to teachers who have the knowledge, skills, and desire to support them in their learning.

We must also find meaningful ways to assess these aspects of schooling. Rather than hold only students accountable for what they know and can do, let us also hold educators, communities, and the public accountable for the quality of the education students receive. Without holding our educational systems accountable for that, we have no right to ask more of our students.

Challenge #6: Supporting Teachers and Quality Teaching

Increasingly, studies are revealing that students' learning is impacted powerfully by the expertise of their teachers (Darling-Hammond 2000; National Commission on Teaching and America's Future 1997; Sanders and Rivers 1996). Dramatic improvements in students' learning have been noted in school districts (such as New York City's Community School District #2) that have concentrated their resources on professional development and instructional improvement (Schwartz and Gandal 2000). Findings such as these strongly suggest that investing in supports for quality teaching is a strategy that has great likelihood for improving student learning.

What do these supports look like? As the stories in Chapter 7 reveal, powerful professional learning occurs when teachers get opportunities to think and talk with each other on a sustained basis. Teachers learn when they talk together about the day-to-day life of their classrooms, about questions that arise in the course of their practice that trouble, puzzle, or excite them. Teachers learn when they look together at students' work for how it reveals progress toward common goals. Teachers learn when they examine their own teaching practice in relation to standards of professional practice.

Another challenge that we face then is to find ways to build time into school life for educators to engage in these kinds of activities. Some schools have done this by arranging for common preparation periods for groups of teachers, after-school meetings, staff development days, teacher research, study and inquiry groups, partnership activities among schools and teacher education programs, or assessment scoring sessions that involve collective discussion and reflection on student work. When administrators arrange for these kinds of activities to take place, they are actively promoting professionalism. They are acknowledging the never-ending process of learning; that a teacher's learning, like that of a student's, is never finished but is always in the making.

These kinds of teacher learning opportunities provide intellectual nourishment in the midst of the mundane tasks that continually threaten to overwhelm daily school life. These kinds of teacher learning opportunities promote an accountability that is firmer and runs deeper than any test score report can ever provide. These kinds of opportunities help teachers become responsible—to themselves and to each other—for their students' and their own growth. They heighten the probability that both teacher and student learning will continue and flourish throughout a school.

Many schools and districts, however, do not feel able to invest the time and the resources needed to involve faculty in this kind of work. They opt instead for what appear to be safer routes to success: purchasing and mandating whole school programs, designs, or textbook series that hold out the promise of great gains on standardized measures of student achievement.

I know of several districts that have gone this route. Professional development time is devoted to learning how to administer these programs rather than to create inquiry about pedagogy and practice. As a result, faculty become program technicians rather than inquirers of learning who can apply their skills and knowledge to different contexts and individuals.

An especially sad, not uncommon, and sometimes unintended casualty of this approach is what happens to teachers in such schools who have a history of success and innovation. Instead of getting recognized for their effective practices and instead of being used as models of good teaching, these exemplary teachers are often forced, by policies that mandate compliance to programs in the name of whole school coherence, to abandon practices that they do that work. This approach to school improvement leads only to standardization—not the high standards of practice that were intended.

Challenge #7: Working for Standards, Not Standardization

"A coherent view of curriculum, assessment, and teaching is at the core of any vision of effective education" (Darling-Hammond 1997, 211). But no matter how coherent a program may be, it will not improve learning if it is mandated and imposed only from above. Studies of successful change initiatives inform us that *what matters most* needs supports from "below"—opportunities for teachers and administrators to learn, experiment, and adapt programs and ideas to their local or individual contexts (Elmore 1996). Without these kinds of opportunities, changes are rarely sustained beyond the time that external enforcement measures are removed (Berman and McLaughlin 1978; Fullan 1991, 1994; McLaughlin 1987, 1990).

Systemwide initiatives currently popular and being enacted in schools around the country—even ones that have many positive aspects such as literacy blocks, grade-level book studies, whole school curricula—provide us with examples of this phenomenon. These kinds of initiatives have the potential to be helpful because they strengthen the coherence of the school experience for all the children within and across grades. However, the very same initiatives can be harmful if they are imposed as mandates without offering sufficient flexibility for teachers to tailor the initiatives to their own students and teaching styles. If schoolwide initiatives are spelled out in too great detail—dictating what, when, and in what order teachers must do what they do—they risk turning teaching into cookie-cutter recipes that constrain creativity, individuality, and leave little room for the inquiry needed to keep teaching exciting, fresh, and responsive to students.

The same is true for assessment initiatives. Flexibility must be built into assessment systems for different people, places, and contexts to demonstrate how they have achieved common goals. Every person and every place should not be demanded to do exactly the same thing in exactly the same way.

The challenge we face in this regard is to create and to use "standards without standardization" (Darling-Hammond 1997). We need to be careful when trying to achieve coherence, be it across a district or within a school, to provide flexibility for individuals or entities to evolve and use ideas. In implementing any initiative, we need to build into the process continual opportunities for those involved to engage in inquiry, to problem solve, and to customize new ideas to their own circumstances (Fullan 1994).

Challenge #8: Balancing Tensions

Reform efforts historically have focused on changing student achievement from the outside: imposing new requirements, new curriculum, new instructional strategies, new standards and tests. Creating real and lasting change however, requires a much more balanced and nuanced approach—one that recognizes and deals with the complexities of competing tensions; one that maintains a balance between external policies and internal practices; one that builds on the strengths and minimizes the weaknesses of a range of initiatives.

There are many strengths of standards and assessments that have been discussed in this book. Among these are the capacity of standards to provide guidance toward and images of possibility of what quality work can be; the opportunity that standards present to initiate collective conversations and inquiry about shared values, purposes, goals, and expectations; the focus that standards and related assessments place on students, their work, and the teaching and learning process.

Negatives of standards initiatives that need to be minimized have also been reviewed. These include the ways that standards and assessments are being used to reduce teaching and learning to test preparation; the one-size-fits-all approach that confuses standards with standardization, dismantling effective practices in the name of creating coherent programs; the high-stakes consequences that are so tightly coupled with tests designed to monitor progress toward standards.

If these weaknesses of standards initiatives can be minimized and if the strengths can be enhanced, standards-driven work must then be balanced with other strengths found in learner-centered practices. We must balance assessing students for what they know and can do with assessing for who they are as learners; we must balance curriculum development based on content and discipline knowledge with curriculum development based on students' interests and strengths. As we develop teaching strategies, school structures, and assessments, we must balance the needs of the whole with the needs of individual learners and classrooms.

Balancing standards-based work with learner-centered practices unites knowledge of content with knowledge of the learner. The balance is maintained by placing assessments that are supportive of learning at the center of the teaching process. Rich assessments and well-conceived standards—combined with appropriate policies, adequate resources, and supports—can create a powerful link between instruction, assessment, student learning, and professional growth.

Together, this mixture can be a driving force to get us from where we are now to where we want to be.

Meeting the Challenges

The complexities of these issues present challenges that are difficult and sometimes overwhelming to consider. They call on us to rethink and rebuild much of our entire public educational system. The exciting thing about this, however, is that the road maps to our goals are not fully developed; the possibilities of the future are not fully envisioned. And, of course, they cannot ever be because new understandings, directions, and issues only evolve as the work unfolds. The one thing about which we can be certain, however, is that there is much work to be done—work that requires enormous energy, creativity, perseverance, and commitment from all who care about public education.

I have spent my entire adult life working in and around schools with educators, children, their families and communities. In the last few years this work has given me the privilege of visiting hundreds of classrooms and dozens of schools throughout my state and across the nation. In all of that time I have not met a single parent, grandparent, or guardian who did not want the best education for her or his child; I have not encountered a single educator who has not felt a sense of responsibility for the children entrusted to her or his care. In my experiences, I have found that it is not a lack of caring that keeps people from acting on behalf of children's best interests. More often than not, rather, it is a lack of understanding about the complexities of the issues, a lack of a sense of empowerment to speak out, or a lack of a feeling of entitlement to be heard that keeps people from getting involved in school improvement initiatives.

This book was written for you, my readers, to help you better understand the issues. Now I call on you to take these understandings and use them to help create better schooling. Who is not better entitled to affect educational policies than those who are closest to children and their learning? Who is more knowledgeable about the impact of educational policies and programs on children than those who devote their lives to nurturing learning?

At this juncture in the current standards-based movement to improve public education, it is time for educators, parents, and concerned citizens to pause and consider how the work is proceeding—to reaffirm what we value, to speak out about the problems, and to work together to readjust the path toward education that enables powerful learning. It is time to remove education from the realm of the media, the power of politics, and service only to the economy; to firmly join our schools with teaching and learning as defined by professional knowledge and practice.

Let us advocate together for teaching that encourages the excitement of understanding new ideas. Let us advocate for the creation of school communities that enable this kind of learning to take place—schools that encourage our students to think critically and to apply their knowledge in the world; schools that respect the various ways that different kinds of people learn; schools that motivate students to want to learn and that inspire them to care about each other; schools that help everyone feel safe enough to take the risks that are necessary for genuine learning to occur.

Let us advocate for this kind of learning to be available for *all* children, regardless of the circumstances to which they are born. Let us advocate for, indeed be vigilant about, establishing standards, assessments, and accountability systems that are in service to these goals. For it is these ideas, practices, and goals that are *the heart of the matter* of schooling.

I have great hopes that the ideas can be realized and that the practices can be brought to life. Indeed, I have already seen this happening in classrooms and schools all over our nation.

The great anthropologist Margaret Mead once said:

Never doubt that . . . thoughtful, committed citizens can change the world: Indeed, it's the only thing that ever has.

I too believe that this is true. We *can* make a difference and change the world if we combine our efforts and stay focused on what matters. We *can* change and improve our schools if we tackle the problems in all of their complexities, balance the tensions of different perspectives, work hard and stay the long haul, and use standards and assessments to learn. In this way we will be able to create better schools that offer *all* children opportunities to reach their potentials and to realize their dreams. We owe our children nothing less.

Using Standards and Assessments in the Service of Learning

Below are suggestions for what educational leaders, teachers, parents, and community members can do to strengthen teaching and learning and its relationship to standards and assessments (Darling-Hammond and Ball 1999; Heubert and Hauser 1999; International Reading Association 1999).

What Educational Leaders Can Do
- *Use standards as a guide, not a recipe, for teaching* within and across grades.
- *Invest in teacher learning rather than teacher-proof programs.* Provide opportunities for teachers to talk about work in relation to standards, what learning environments they are creating to ensure that the standards are being met, and what teaching strategies are effective.
- *Mobilize resources for students in need of supports rather than punish them through tracking or retention.* Establish tutoring programs, small-group work, after-school and summer programs, rich learning activities (museums, trips, projects, activities, etc.).
- *Avoid sanctions and rewards to teachers and students.* Highlight successful teacher practices and student work as models of possibility for what others can do.
- *Use multiple forms of evidence to make important decisions about students' futures.* Do not rely on the results of a single test for high-stakes decisions.
- *Focus attention, resources, and time on meaningful learning rather than on teaching to the test.* Encourage test preparation that familiarizes students with the format of tests rather than test preparation that replaces rich learning experiences.

What Teachers Can Do
- *Make sure that your practice embodies clear goals, values, and standards.* Get comfortable talking about how what you do reflects these values, goals, and standards.
- *Create rich learning environments in your classroom* that utilize knowledge of how children learn, that are responsive to children's interests and needs, and that emphasize understanding and the application of knowledge.
- *Develop rich assessments* and systems of assessment that include multiple forms of evidence and that enhance and inform learning by documenting (1) *what* students know and can do in relation to valued goals, as well as (2) *how* students go about their learning.

(Continued on page 168)

Figure 8–1   ©2000 by Beverly Falk from *The Heart of the Matter*. Portsmouth. NH: Heinemann

- *Take responsibility for educating families, the community, and policy makers* about how children learn, what kind of environments best support that learning, and the types of assessments that best inform teaching and support student learning.
- *Be ethical about how you relate to tests.* Resist spending inordinate amounts of time doing test preparation at the expense of meaningful learning; do not take actions to improve test scores (prompting or changing answers, coaching students in advance on questions that will appear on test) that are not related to helping students to learn better; do not focus on some students at the expense of others so that they can do better on tests and raise overall averages.
- *Inform families and the community about test results.*

What Parents and Community Members Can Do
- *Find out* about the educational program and the role of testing and other forms of assessment in your child's school.
- *Speak up* about the impact that high-stakes testing has on your child.
- *Advocate for information* about your child's learning that can be useful to supporting his or her learning.

Figure 8–1.   (Continued)   ©2000 by Beverly Falk from *The Heart of the Matter*, Portsmouth, NH: Heinemann

References

Allen, D. 1998. *Assessing Student Learning: From Grading to Understanding*. New York: Teachers College Press.

Allington, R. L., and A. McGill-Franzen. 1992. "Unintended Effects of Educational Reform in New York." *Educational Policy* 6: 397–414.

Alvarado, A. 1998. "Professional Development *Is* the Job." *American Educator* 22 (4): 18–23.

American Educational Research Association (AERA), American Psychological Association (APA), National Council on Measurement in Education (NCME). 1999. *Standards for Educational and Psychological Testing*. Washington, DC: AERA.

American Federation of Teachers. 1997. *Making Standards Matter: An Annual Fifty-State Report on Efforts to Raise Academic Standards*. Washington, DC: American Federation of Teachers.

Apple, M. 1995. "The Politics of a National Curriculum." In *Transforming Schools*, edited by P. Cookson and B. Schneider. New York: Garland Publishing.

Archbald, D. A., and F. M. Newmann. 1988. *Beyond Standardized Testing: Assessing Authentic Academic Achievement in the Secondary School*. Reston, VA: National Association of Secondary School Principals.

Baratz-Snowden, J. 1993. "Opportunity to Learn: Implications for Professional Development." *Journal of Negro Education* 6 (23): 311–23.

Barrs, M., S. Ellis, H. Hester, and A. Thomas. 1988. *The Primary Language/Learning Record*. London: ILEA/Centre for Language in Primary Education.

Bensman, D. 1994. *Lives of the Graduates of Central Park East Elementary School: Where Have They Gone? What Did They Really Learn?* New York: National Center for Restructuring Education, Schools, and Teaching (NCREST).

Berlak, H. 1995. "Culture, Imperialism, and Goals 2000." In *Educational Freedom in a Democratic Society*, edited by R. Miller. Brandon, VT: Holistic Education Press.

Berman, P., and M. W. McLaughlin. 1978. *Federal Programs Supporting Educational Change: Vol. 8. Implementing and Sustaining Innovations*. Santa Monica, CA: Rand.

Boyer, E. 1983. *High School*. New York: Harper and Row.

———. 1995. *The Basic School: A Community for Learning*. San Francisco: Jossey-Bass.

Bruner, J. 1960. *The Process of Education*. Cambridge, MA: Harvard University Press.

Byrnes, D., and K. Yamamoto. 1986. "Views on Grade Repetition." *Journal of Research and Development in Education* 20: 14–20.

Calkins, L., K. Montgomery, D. Santman, and B. Falk. 1998. *A Teacher's Guide to Standardized Reading Tests: Knowledge Is Power*. Portsmouth, NH: Heinemann.

Cannell, J. J. 1987. *Nationally Normed Elementary Achievement Testing in America's Public Schools: How All Fifty Are Above the National Average*. Naniels, WV: Friends for Education.

———. 1989. *How Public Educators Cheat on Standardized Achievement Tests*. Albuquerque: Friends for Education.

Carini, P. 1986. "Building from Children's Strengths." *Journal of Education* 168: 13–24.

———. 1987. *On Value in Education*. New York: The City College Workshop Center.

Carnegie Council on Adolescent Development. 1989. *Turning Points: Preparing Youth for the Twenty-First Century*. New York: Carnegie Corporation of New York.

Chase, B. 2000. "A Sucker Punch: Standards, High-Stakes Tests, and the Unlevel Playing Field." *Education Week* 19 (Jan. 19): 44.

Chittenden, E., and R. Courtney. 1989. "Assessment of Young Children's Reading: Documentation as an Alternative to Testing." In *Emerging Literacy: Young Children Learn to Read and Write*, edited by D. S. Strickland and L. M. Morrow, 107–20. Newark, DE: International Reading Association.

Clotfeller, C., and H. Ladd. 1996. "Recognizing and Rewarding Success in Public Schools." In *Holding Schools Accountable: Performance-Based Reform in Education*, edited by H. Ladd. Washington, DC: Brookings Institution.

Cohen, D. K., and C. A. Barnes. 1993. Conclusion: "A New Pedagogy for Policy." In *Teaching for Understanding: Challenges for Policy and Practice*, edited by D. K. Cohen, M. W. McLaughlin, and J. E. Talbert, 240–75. San Francisco: Jossey-Bass.

Cohen, D. K., M. W. McLaughlin, and J. E. Talbert, eds. 1993. *Teaching for Understanding: Challenges for Policy and Practice*. San Francisco: Jossey-Bass.

Cohen, D. H., V. Stern, and N. Balaban. 1997. *Observing and Recording the Behavior of Young Children*. 4th ed. New York: Teachers College Press.

Cohen, M. 1980. *First Grade Takes a Test*. New York: Greenwillow.

Cooper, E., and J. Sherk. 1989. "Addressing Urban School Reform: Issues and Alliances." *Journal of Negro Education* 58 (3): 315–31.

Darling-Hammond, L. 1989. "Curiouser and Curiouser: Alice in Testingland." *Rethinking Schools* 3: 1, 17.

———. 1991. "The Implications of Testing Policy for Educational Quality and Equality." *Phi Delta Kappan* 73: 220–25.

————. 1993. "Reframing the School Reform Agenda: Developing Capacity for School Transformation." *Phi Delta Kappan* 74: 753–61.

————. 1994a. "National Standards and Assessments: Will They Improve Education?" *American Journal of Education* 102 (4): 478–510.

————. 1994b. "Performance-Based Assessment and Educational Equity." *Harvard Educational Review* 54: 5–30.

————. 1995. "Inequality and Access to Knowledge." In *Handbook of Research on Multicultural Education*, edited by J. Banks, 465–83. Old Tappan: NJ: Macmillan.

————. 1997. *The Right to Learn: A Blueprint for School Reform*. New York: Jossey-Bass.

————. 2000. "Teacher Quality and Student Achievement: A Review of State Policy Evidence." *Education Policy Analysis Archives*, January. <www.Epaa.asu.edu>.

Darling-Hammond, L., J. Ancess, and B. Falk. 1995. *Authentic Assessment in Action*. New York: Teachers College Press.

Darling-Hammond, L., and D. L. Ball. 1999. *Teaching for High Standards: What Policymakers Need to Know and Be Able to Do*. New York: National Commission on Teaching and America's Future and Consortium for Policy Research in Education.

Darling-Hammond, L., L. Einbender, F. Frelow, and J. Ley-King. 1993. *Authentic Assessment in Practice: A Collection of Portfolios, Performance Tasks, Exhibitions, and Documentation*. New York: National Center for Restructuring Education, Schools, and Teaching (NCREST).

Darling-Hammond, L., and B. Falk. 1997a. "Policy for Authentic Assessment." In *Assessment for Equity and Inclusion*, edited by A. Lin Goodwin. London: Routledge.

————. 1997b. "Using Standards and Assessments to Support Student Learning." *Phi Delta Kappan* 79: 190–99.

Darling-Hammond, L., and A. Wise. 1985. "Beyond Standardization: State Standards and School Improvement." *The Elementary School Journal* 85: 315–36.

Dewey, J. 1916. *Democracy and Education*. New York: Macmillan.

Dorfman, A. 1997. Teachers' Understanding of Performance Assessment. Paper presented at the annual meeting of the American Educational Research Association, Chicago, Illinois, March.

Du Bois, W. E. B. 1970. "The Freedom to Learn." In *W. E. B. Du Bois Speaks*, edited by P. S. Foner, pp. 230–31. New York: Pathfinder.

Duckworth, E. 1987. *The "Having of Wonderful Ideas" and Other Essays*. New York: Teachers College Press.

Eckstein, M., and H. Noah. 1993. *Secondary School Examinations*. New Haven: Yale University Press.

Edelsky, C., and S. Harman. 1988. "One More Critique of Reading Tests—With Two Differences." *English Education* 20: 157–71.

Education USA. 1999. "Critics: Old Style Tests May Hamper School Reform." *Education USA*, 19 April, 1, 3.

Educational Testing Service. 1989a. *Crossroads in American Education.* Princeton, NJ: Educational Testing Service.

————. 1989b. *A World of Difference: An International Assessment of Mathematics and Science.* Princeton, NJ: Educational Testing Service.

————. 1990. *Learning to Write in Our Nation's Schools: Instruction and Achievement in 1988 at Grades 4, 8, and 12.* Princeton, NJ: Educational Testing Service.

Edwards, C., L. Gandini, and G. Forman, eds. 1998. *The Hundred Languages of Children: The Reggio Emilia Approach—Advanced Reflections.* Greenwich, CT: Ablex Publishing.

Elbow, P. 1986. *Embracing Contraries and Explorations in Learning and Teaching.* New York: Oxford University Press.

Elmore, R. 1983. "Complexity and Control: What Legislators and Administrators Can Do About Implementing Policy." In *Handbook of Teaching and Policy*, edited by L. S. Shulman and G. Sykes, pp. 342–69. White Plains, NY: Longman.

————. 1996. "Getting to Scale with Good Educational Practice." *Harvard Educational Review* 66 (1): 1–26.

Elmore, R., C. Abelmann, and S. Fuhrman. 1996. "The New Accountability in State Education Reform: From Process to Performance." In *Holding Schools Accountable: Performance-Based Reform in Education*, edited by H. Ladd, pp. 65–98. Washington, DC: Brookings Institution.

Falk, B. 1993. The Learner at the Center of the Curriculum: A Case Study of the Process of Developing a Learner-Centered Curriculum. Unpublished doctoral dissertation.

————. 1994. *The Bronx New School: Weaving Assessment into the Fabric of Teaching and Learning.* New York: National Center for Restructuring Education, Schools, and Teaching (NCREST).

————. 1996. "Teaching the Way Children Learn." In *Teacher Learning*, edited by M. McLaughlin and I. Oberman. New York: Teacher College Press.

————. 1998. "Testing the Way Students Learn: Principles for Valid Literacy Assessments." *Language Arts* 76 (1): 57–66.

————. 1999. *Reframing the Basics of Education: A Report on the Work of the Basic School.* New York: National Center for Restructuring Education, Schools, and Teaching (NCREST).

Falk, B., and L. Darling-Hammond. 1993. *The Primary Language Record at P.S. 261: How Assessment Transforms Teaching and Learning.* New York: National Center for Restructuring Education, Schools, and Teaching (NCREST).

Falk, B., and J. Larson. 1995. An Invitation to Invention: Top-down Support for Bottom-up Reform of Assessment in New York State. Paper presented at the annual meeting of the American Educational Research Association, April, San Francisco.

Falk, B., S. MacMurdy, and L. Darling-Hammond. 1995. *Taking a Different Look: How the Primary Language Record Supports Teaching for Diverse Learners.* New York: National Center for Restructuring Education, Schools, and Teaching (NCREST).

Falk, B., R. Mann, and L. Scorsone. In press. "Professional Learning Through Participation in the National Board of Professional Teaching Standards Certification Process. *American Educator.*

Falk, B., and S. Ort. 1998. "Sitting Down to Score: Teacher Learning Through Assessment." *Phi Delta Kappan* 80 (1): 59–64.

———. 1999. *Technical Report on the Early Literacy Profile.* New York: National Center for Restructuring Education, Schools, and Teaching (NCREST).

Firestone, W., D. Mayrowetz, and H. Fairman. 1997. Rethinking High Stakes: External Obligation in Assessment Policy. Paper presented at the annual meeting of the American Educational Research Association, April, Chicago, Illinois.

Fitzgerald, F. 1979. *America Revised.* New York: Vintage Books.

Fosnot, C. T. 1989. *Enquiring Teachers, Enquiring Learners.* New York: Teachers College Press.

Fraiberg, S. 1959. *The Magic Years: Understanding and Handling the Problems of Early Childhood.* New York: Charles Scribner's Sons.

Freire, P. 1973. *Pedagogy of the Oppressed.* New York: Seabury Press.

Fullan, M. 1991. *The New Meaning of Educational Change.* New York: Teachers College Press.

———. 1994. Turning Systemic Thinking on Its Head. Paper prepared for the U.S. Department of Education.

Gagnon, P. 1994. "The Case for Standards: Equity and Competence." *Journal of Education* 176 (3): 1–16.

Gampert, R., and P. Opperman. 1988. Longitudinal Study of the 1982–83 "Promotional Gates Students." Paper presented at the annual meeting of the American Educational Research Association, April, 1994, New Orleans.

Garcia, G. E., and P. D. Pearson. 1994. "Assessment and Diversity." In *Review of Research in Education 20*, edited by L. Darling-Hammond, 337–91. Washington, DC: American Educational Research Association (AERA).

Gardner, H. 1983. *Frames of Mind: The Theory of Multiple Intelligences.* New York: Basic Books.

Giroux, H. A. 1988. *Teachers as Intellectuals: Toward a Critical Pedagogy of Learning.* Granby, MA: Bergin and Garvey.

Glaser, R., and E. Silver. 1994. "Assessment, Testing, and Instruction: Retrospect and Prospect." *Review of Research in Education 20,* edited by L. Darling-Hammond, 393–419. Washington, DC: American Educational Research Association.

Goodlad, J. 1984. *A Place Called School: Prospects for the Future.* New York: McGraw-Hill.

Gordon, E. 1999. *Reflections from the Back of the Bus.* New York: Teachers College Press.

Greene, M. 1978. *Landscapes of Learning.* New York: Teachers College Press.

Haney, W., and G. Madaus. 1986. Effects of Standardized Testing and the Future of the National Assessment of Educational Progress. Working paper for the NAEP study group. Chestnut Hill, MA: Boston College, Center for the Study of Testing, Evaluation, and Educational Policy.

Harmon, S. 1996. "New Life for Old Tests." *Thrust for Educational Leadership* (May/June): 20–23.

Harris, D. E., and J. F. Carr. 1996. *How to Use Standards in the Classroom.* Alexandria, VA: Association for Supervision and Curriculum Development.

Harris, J., and J. Sammons. 1989. *Failing Our Children: How Standardized Tests Damage New York's Youngest Students.* New York: New York Public Interest Group.

Hawkins, D. 1965. "Messing About in Science." *Science and Children* 2 (5).

Hemingway, E. 1952. *Old Man and the Sea.* New York: Scribner.

Herman, J., P. Aschbacher, and L. Winters. 1992. *A Practical Guide to Alternative Assessment.* Alexandria, VA: Association for Supervision and Curriculum Development.

Heubert, J. P., and R. M. Hauser. 1999. *High Stakes: Testing for Tracking, Promotion, and Graduation.* Washington, DC: National Academy Press.

Hill, C. 1992. *Testing and Assessment: An Ecological Approach.* New York: Teachers College Press.

Hirsch, E. D. Jr. 1996. *The Schools We Need and Why We Don't Have Them.* New York: Doubleday.

Hoff, D. J. 1999. "Standards at Crossroads After Decade." *Education Week* 19 (Sept. 2): 1, 9.

Holmes, C. T., and K. M. Matthews. 1984. "The Effects of Nonpromotion on Elementary and Junior High School Pupils: A Meta-Analysis." *Review of Educational Research* 54: 225–36.

Holmes Group. 1986. *Tomorrow's Teachers: A Report of the Holmes Group*. East Lansing, MI: Holmes Group.

International Reading Association. 1999. High-Stakes Assessments in Reading: A Position Statement of the International Reading Association. *The Reading Teacher* 53 (3): 257–64.

Jackson, S. 1993. "Opportunity to Learn: The Health Connection." *Journal of Negro Education* 62 (3): 377–93.

Jannes, E. 1995. Paper prepared for course on performance assessment.

Jones, K., and B. L. Whitford. 1997. "Kentucky's Conflicting Reform Principles: High-Stakes School Accountability and Student Performance Assessment." *Phi Delta Kappan* 79 (4): 276–81.

Kamii, C. 1985. *Young Children Reinvent Arithmetic*. New York: Teachers College Press.

———. 1989. *Young Children Continue to Reinvent Arithmetic*. New York: Teachers College Press.

Kamin, L. 1974. *The Science and Politics of IQ*. New York: Wiley.

Kantrowitz, B., and P. Wingert. 1989. "How Kids Learn." *Newsweek* (April 17): 50–57.

Kappner, A. S. 1999. "Standards and Assessment: Progressive Educators Respond." *Street Scenes* (Fall): 2, 12.

Kates, L. 1999. Performance Assessment and Two Teachers' Learning: A Model of Possibility. Unpublished paper.

Kelley, B. 1998. "An Era of Teacher Leadership." *Teacher to Teacher* 9 (March): 2.

Kohn, A. 1999. *The Schools Our Children Deserve: Moving Beyond Traditional Classrooms and "Tougher Standards."* Boston: Houghton Mifflin.

Koretz, D. 1988. "Arriving in Lake Wobegon: Are Standardized Tests Exaggerating Achievement and Distorting Instruction?" *American Educator* 12 (2): 8–15, 46–52.

———. 1996. *Summary of Findings: Technical Advisory Group for the New York State New Assessments Project*. New York: National Center for Restructuring Education, Schools, and Teaching (NCREST).

Kornhaber, M., and H. Gardner. 1993. *Varieties of Excellence: Identifying and Assessing Children's Talents*. New York: National Center for Restructuring Education, Schools, and Teaching (NCREST).

Kozol, J. 1991. *Savage Inequalities: Children in America's Schools*. New York: HarperCollins.

Lee, V. E., and A. Bryk. 1988. "Curriculum Tracking as Mediating the Social Distribution of High School Achievement." *Sociology of Education* 61: 78–94.

Lewy, A. 1996. "Postmodernism in the Field of Achievement Testing." *Studies in Educational Evaluation* 22: 233–44.

Lieberman, A. 1995. "Practices That Support Teacher Development: Transforming Conceptions of Professional Learning." *Phi Delta Kappan* 76 (8): 591–96.

Lieberman, A., and M. A. McLaughlin. 1992. "Networks for Educational Change: Powerful and Problematic." *Phi Delta Kappan* 7 (39): 673–77.

Linn, R. L. 1987. "Accountability: The Comparison of Educational Systems and the Quality of Test Results." *Educational Policy* 1: 181–98.

———. 1996. *Summary of Findings: Technical Advisory Group for the New York State New Assessments Project*. New York: National Center for Restructuring Education, Schools, and Teaching (NCREST).

Linn, R. L., E. L. Baker, and S. B. Dunbar. 1991. "Complex, Performance-Based Assessments: Expectations and Validation Criteria." *Educational Researcher* 20: 15–21.

Little, J. W. 1992. "Teacher Development and Educational Policy." In *Teacher Development and Educational Change*, edited by M. Fullan and A. Hargreaves, 170–93. London: Falmer Press.

———. 1993. *Teachers' Professional Development in a Climate of Educational Reform*. New York: National Center for Restructuring Education, Schools, and Teaching (NCREST).

Maduas, G. F. 1989. "The Distortion of Teaching and Testing: High Stakes Testing and Instruction." *Peabody Journal of Education* 65 (3).

Madaus, G. F., T. Kellaghan, E. A. Rakow, and D. J. King. 1992. *The Influence of Testing on Teaching Math and Science in Grades 4–12*. Chestnut Hill, MA: Boston College, Center for the Study of Testing, Evaluation, and Educational Policy.

Marzano, R., and J. Kendall. 1996. *Designing Standards-Based Districts, Schools, and Classrooms*. Aurora, CO: Mid-Continent Regional Educational Laboratory.

Massachusetts Advocacy Center and the Center for Early Adolescence. 1988. *Before It's Too Late: Dropout Prevention in the Middle Grades*. Boston: Massachusetts Advocacy Center and the Center for Early Adolescence.

McCloskey, R. 1950. *Blueberries for Sal*. New York: Puffin.

McCombs, B., and J. S. Whisler. 1997. *The Learner-Centered Classroom and School: Strategies for Increasing Student Motivation and Achievement*. San Francisco: Jossey-Bass.

McDermott, M. 1999. "Board Enforces Test Practice." *The Riverdale Press*, 2 September, A3.

McDonald, J. 1996. *Redesigning School: Lessons for the Twenty-First Century*. San Francisco: Jossey-Bass.

McDonald, J., S. Smith, D. Turner, M. Finney, and E. Barton. 1993. *Graduation by Exhibition*. Alexandra, VA: Association for Supervision and Curriculum Development.

McGill-Franzen, A., and R. L. Allington. 1993. "Flunk 'em or Get Them Classified: The Contamination of Primary Grade Accountability Data." *Educational Researcher* 22: 19–22.

McKnight, C. C., F. J. Crosswhite, J. A. Dossey, E. Kifer, J. O. Swafford, K. J. Travers, and T. J. Cooney. 1987. *The Underachieving Curriculum: Assessing U.S. School Mathematics from an International Perspective*. Champaign, IL: Stipes.

McLaughlin, M. W. 1987. "Learning from Experience: Lessons from Policy Implementation." *Educational Evaluation and Policy Analysis* 92: 171–78.

———. 1990. "The RAND Change Agent Study Revisited: Macro Perspectives and Micro Realities." *Educational Researcher* 19 (9): 11–16.

Meier, D. 1992. "Reinventing Teaching." *Teachers College Record* 93 (4): 594–609.

Meisels, S., F. Liaw, A. Dorfman, and R. Fails. 1993. The Work Sampling System: Reliability and Validity of a Performance Assessment for Young Children. Paper presented at the annual meeting of the American Educational Research Association, April, Atlanta, Georgia.

Miller, J. 1990. Educational Transitions. Unpublished master's thesis, Sarah Lawrence College, Bronxville, New York.

Mistral, G. 1946. Llamado por el nino. The Call for the Child. Oral presentation to the United Nations, New York City, New York.

Mitchell, R. 1992. *Testing for Learning: How New Approaches to Evaluation Can Improve American Schools*. New York: The Free Press.

Moll, L. C., and J. Greenberg. 1990. "Creating Zones of Possibilities: Combining Social Contexts for Instruction." In *Vygotsky and Education*, edited by L. C. Moll, 319–48. Cambridge, England: Cambridge University Press.

Moss, P. A. 1994. "Can There Be Validity Without Reliability?" *Educational Researcher* 23: 5–12.

Murnane, R., and F. Levy. 1996. "Teaching New Standards." In *Rewards and Reform: Creating Educational Incentives That Work*, edited by S. Fuhrman and J. O'Day, 257–93. San Francisco: Jossey-Bass.

National Assessment of Educational Progress (NAEP). 1981. *Reading, Thinking, and Writing: Results from the 1979–1980 National Assessment of Reading and Literature*. Denver: National Assessment of Educational Progress.

National Association for the Education of Young Children. 1988. "NAEYC Position Statement on Developmentally Appropriate Practice in the Primary Grades, Serving 5- Through 8-Year-Olds." *Young Children* (January): 64–84.

———. 1991. "Guidelines for Appropriate Curriculum Content and Assessment in Programs Serving Children Ages 3 Through 8." *Young Children* 46 (3): 21–38.

National Association of State Boards of Education. 1988. *Right from the Start: The Report of the NASBE Task Force on Early Childhood Education.* Alexandria, VA: National Association of State Boards of Education.

National Center for Fair and Open Testing. 1999. *Fairtest Examiner* 13 (2).

National Commission on Excellence in Education. 1983. *A Nation at Risk: The Imperative for Educational Reform.* Washington, DC: U.S. Government Printing Office.

National Commission on Teaching and America's Future. 1996. *What Matters Most: Teaching for America's future.* New York: National Commission on Teaching and America's Future.

———. 1997. *Doing What Matters Most: Investing in Quality Teaching.* New York: National Commission on Teaching and America's Future.

National Council of Teachers of English. 1999. *On Testing and Equitable Treatment of Students.* <www.ncte.org>.

National Council of Teachers of Mathematics. 1989. *Curriculum and Evaluation Standards for School Mathematics.* Reston, VA: NCTM.

National Council on Education, Standards, and Testing. 1992. *Raising Standards for American Education.* Washington, DC: National Council on Education, Standards, and Testing.

National Education Goals Panel. 1991. *The National Education Goals Report: Building a Nation of Learners.* Washington, DC: National Education Goals Panel.

National Forum on Assessment. 1995. *Principles and Indicators for Student Assessment Systems.* Cambridge, MA: National Center for Fair and Open Testing.

National Research Council. 1982. *Ability Testing: Uses, Consequences, and Controversies,* edited by A. K. Wigdor and W. R. Garner. Washington, DC: National Academy Press.

Newmann, F., ed. 1996. *Authentic Achievement: Restructuring Schools for Intellectual Quality.* San Francisco: Jossey-Bass.

New York State Curriculum and Assessment Council. 1994. *Learning-Centered Curriculum and Assessment for New York State.* Albany: New York State Education Department.

———. 1997. *New York State: The State of Learning.* Albany: New York State Education Department.

———. 1999. *The Early Literacy Profile: An Assessment Instrument.* Albany: New York State Education Department.

Noble, J. A., and M. L. Smith. 1994. Old and New Beliefs About Measurement-Driven Reform: "The More Things Change, the More They Remain the Same." *CSE Technical Report 373.* Los Angeles: National Center for Research on Evaluation, Standards, and Student Testing.

Oakes, J. 1985. *Keeping Track: How Schools Structure Inequality*. New Haven: Yale University Press.

———. 1990. *Multiplying Inequalities: The Effects of Race, Social Class, and Tracking on Opportunities to Learn Mathematics and Science*. Santa Monica, CA: Rand.

Office of Research, U.S. Department of Education. 1993, April. *What's Wrong with Writing and What Can We Do Right Now?* Education research report. Washington, DC: U.S. Department of Education.

Ohanian, Susan. 1999. *One Size Fits Few*. Portsmouth, NH: Heinemann.

O'Neil, J., and C. Tell. 1999. "Why Students Lose When 'Tougher Standards' Win." *Educational Leadership* 57 (1): 18–22.

Orfield, G. F., and C. Ashkinaze. 1991. *The Closing Door: Conservative Policy and Black Opportunity*. Chicago: University of Chicago Press.

Ort, S. 1999. Standards in Practice: A Study of a New York City High School's Struggle for Excellence and Equity and Its Relationship to Policy. Unpublished doctoral dissertation.

Perrone, V. 1999. *What Should We Make of Standards?* New York: Bank Street College of Education.

Perrone, V, ed. 1991. *Expanding Student Assessment*. Alexandria, VA: Association for Supervision and Curriculum Development.

Piaget, J., and B. Inhelder. 1970. *The Science of Education and the Psychology of the Child*. New York: Penguin Books.

Porter, A. 1995. "The Uses and Misuses of Opportunity-to-Learn Standards." *Educational Researcher* 24 (1): 21–27.

Porter, G. 1995. "The White Man's Burden." In *Educational Freedom in a Democratic Society*, edited by R. Miller. Brandon, VT: Holistic Education Press.

Price, J., S. Schwabacher, and E. Chittenden. 1993. *The Multiple Forms of Evidence Study*. New York: National Center for Restructuring Education, Schools, and Teaching (NCREST).

Prospect Center. 1986. *The Prospect Center Documentary Processes: In Progress*. North Bennington, VT: The Prospect Archive and Center for Education and Research.

Purpel, D. 1995. "Goals 2000: The Triumph of Vulgarity and the Legitimization of Social Injustice." In *Educational Freedom in a Democratic Society*, edited by R. Miller. Brandon, VT: Holistic Education Press.

Ravitch, D., ed. 1995. *Debating the Future of American Education*. Washington, DC: Brookings Institution.

Resnick, L. B. 1987. *Education and Learning to Think*. Washington, DC: National Academy Press.

————. 1994. "Performance Puzzles." *American Journal of Education* 102 (August): 511–26.

————. 1995. "Standards for Education." In *Debating the Future of American Standards*, edited by D. Ravitch. Washington, DC: Brookings Institution.

Resnick, L. B., and M. W. Hall. 1998. "Learning Organizations for Sustainable Educational Reform." *Daedalus* 127 (4): 89–118.

Resnick, L. B., and D. P. Resnick. 1991. "Assessing the Thinking Curriculum: New Tools for Educational Reform." In *Changing Assessments: Alternative Views of Aptitude, Achievement, and Instruction*, edited by B. G. Gifford and M. C. O'Connor. Boston: Kluwer Academic Publishers.

Rothman, R. 1995. *Measuring Up: Standards, Assessment, and School Reform*. San Francisco: Jossey-Bass.

————. 1997. *Organizing Schools So That All Children Can Learn*. New York: National Center on Education and the Economy.

Sanders, W. L., and J. C. Rivers. 1996. *Cumulative and Residual Effects of Teachers on Future Student Academic Achievement*. Knoxville: University of Tennessee Value-Added Research and Assessment Center.

Schmidt, W., C. McKnight, and S. Raizen. 1996. *A Splintered Vision*. Boston: Kluwer Academic Publishers.

Schoenfeld, A. H. 1988. "When Good Teaching Leads to Bad Results: The Disasters of 'Well Taught' Mathematics Courses." *Educational Psychologist* 23 (2): 145–66.

Schwartz, R., and M. Gandal. 2000. "Don't Shoot the Messenger." *Education Week* 19 (Jan. 19): 40–41, 60.

Seidel, S. 1998. "Wondering to Be Done: The Collaborative Assessment Conference." In *Assessing Student Learning: From Grading to Understanding*, edited by D. Allen, 21–39. New York: Teachers College Press.

Sheingold, K., J. I. Heller, and S. T. Paulukonis. 1995. *Actively Seeking Evidence: Teacher Change Through Assessment Development*. Center for Performance Assessment Report MS #94–04. Princeton, NJ: Educational Testing Service.

Sheingold, K., J. I. Heller, and B. A. Storms. 1997. On the Mutual Influence of Teachers' Professional Development and Assessment Quality in Curricular Reform. Paper presented at the annual meeting of the American Educational Research Association, Chicago, April.

Shepard, L. 1995. "Using Assessment to Improve Learning." *Educational Leadership* 52: 38–43.

Shepard, L., and M. L. Smith. 1986. "Synthesis of Research on School Readiness and Kindergarten Retention." *Educational Leadership* (Nov.): 78–86.

Sizer, T. 1995. "Will National Standards and Assessments Make a Difference?" In *Debating the Future of American Education*, edited by D. Ravitch. Washington, DC: Brookings Institution.

Skinner, B. F. 1954. "The Science of Learning and the Art of Teaching." *Harvard Educational Review* 24: 86–97.

Smith, M. L., and C. Rottenberg. 1991. "Unintended Consequences of External Testing in Elementary Schools." *Educational Measurement: Issues and Practices*: 7–11.

Sprenger, M. 1999. *Learning and Memory: The Brain in Action*. Alexandria, VA: Association for Supervision and Curriculum Development.

Steinberg, A., K. Cushman, and R. Riordan. 1999. *Schooling for the Real World: A Guide to Providing Enriching Classroom Learning Experiences*. San Francisco: Jossey-Bass.

Sternberg, R. J. 1985. *Beyond IQ*. New York: Cambridge University Press.

Stiggins, R. J. 1997. *Student-Centered Classroom Assessment*. 2d ed. Paramus, NJ: Merrill.

Stoskopf, A. 2000. "Clio's Lament." *Education Week* 20 (Feb. 2): 38, 41.

Tate, W. 1994. "Mathematics Standards and Urban Education: Is This the Road to Recovery?" *Educational Forum* 58: 380–90.

Thomas, W., B. Storms, K. Sheingold, J. Heller, J. Paulukonis, A. Nunez, and J. Wing. 1995. *California Learning Assessment System Portfolio Assessment Research and Development Project: Final Report*. Princeton, NJ: Center for Performance Assessment, Educational Testing Service.

Thompson, S. 1999. "Confessions of a 'Standardisto.'" *Education Week* 19 (October 6): 46.

Trimble, K., and R. L. Sinclair. 1986. Ability Grouping and Differing Conditions for Learning: An Analysis of Content and Instruction in Ability-Grouped Classes. Paper presented at the annual meeting of the American Educational Research Association, San Francisco, April.

Tyack, D. 1974. *The One Best System: A History of American Urban Education*. Cambridge, MA: Harvard University Press.

Tyler, R. 1949. *Basic Principles of Curriculum and Instruction*. Chicago: University of Chicago Press.

Tucker, M., and J. Codding. 1998. *Standards for Our Schools: How to Set Them, Measure Them, and Reach Them*. San Francisco: Jossey-Bass.

Valencia, S., E. Hiebert, and P. Afflerbach. 1994. *Authentic Reading Assessment: Practices and Possibilities*. Newark, DE: International Reading Association.

Vygotsky, L. S. 1978. *Mind in Society*. Cambridge, MA: Harvard University Press.

Wasley, P., R. Hampel, and R. Clark. 1997. *Kids and School Reform*. San Francisco: Jossey-Bass.

Weber, L. 1991. *Inquiry, Noticing, Joining with, and Following After*. New York: The City College Workshop Center.

Wehlage, G. G., R. A. Rutter, G. A. Smith, N. Lesko, and R. R. Fernandez. 1989. *Reducing the Risk: Schools as Communities of Support*. Bristol, PA: Falmer Press.

White House Initiative on Educational Excellence for Hispanic Americans. 1999. *A Report to the Nation: Policies and Issues on Testing Hispanic Students in the United States*. Washington, DC: White House Initiative on Educational Excellence for Hispanic Americans.

White, K. A., and R. C. Johnston. 1999. "Summer School: Amid Successes, Concerns Persist." *Education Week* 19 (Sept. 22): 1, 8–9.

Wiggins, G. 1989. "A True Test: Toward More Authentic and Equitable Assessment." *Phi Delta Kappan* 70: 703–13.

———. 1993. *Assessing Student Performance: Exploring the Purpose and Limits of Testing*. San Francisco: Jossey-Bass.

———. 1998. *Educative Assessment: Designing Assessments to Inform and Improve Student Performance*. San Francisco: Jossey-Bass.

Wiggins, G., and J. McTighe. 1998. *Understanding by Design*. Alexandria, VA: Association for Supervision and Curriculum Development.

Wilson, M. S. 1990. "A Conflict of Interests: The Case of Mark Black." *Educational Evaluation and Policy Analysis* 12 (3): 293–310.

Wiske, M., ed. 1997. *Teaching for Understanding*. San Francisco: Jossey-Bass.

Wolf, D. P. 1989. "Portfolio Assessment: Sampling Student Work." *Educational Leadership* (April): 35–39.

Wood, D., and L. Einbender. 1995. *An Authentic Journey: Emergent Understandings About Authentic Assessment and Authentic Practice*. New York: National Center for Restructuring Education, Schools, and Teaching (NCREST).

Index